**W9-DES-792**

# Hollywood Blackjack

An Uncensored Guide to Doing It Like a Pro

Dave Stann

RGE Publishing, Ltd.
Las Vegas, Nevada

RGE Publishing, Ltd.
Las Vegas, NV
(702) 798-7743
(702) 798-8743 fax
www.rge21.com
books@rge21.com

©2007 by Dave Stann
Printed in the United States of America
15 14 13 12 11 10 09 08 07      1 2 3 4 5

ISBN10: 0-910575-26-6
ISBN13: 978-0-910575-26-3
Library of Congress Control Number: 2007930895

Publishers
Viktor Nacht, Bethany Paige

Cover Design
Joslynn Anderson, Canyon Creative

This book is dedicated to two icons I never had a chance to meet while they were still with us, but who nonetheless influenced my growth as a blackjack player, writer, and artist immeasurably. To Kenny Uston and Hunter S. Thompson, two strange and beautiful fuckers who taught me that although raw talent, intelligence, and creativity are absolute prerequisites, it's ultimately not just *what you know* but rather *how you show it* that truly matters. Thank you for ruining my life — and for setting me free.

Oh yeah, and also, for all my bitches (you know who you are): Your constant love, support, acceptance, trust, tolerance, laughter, advice, patience, compassion, wisdom, warmth, and unwavering faith in me (as well as the occasional handjob, of course) are really what kept my mind in balance, my soul in check, and my fingers typing. I love you from the bottom of my heart, and in case you haven't figured it out by now: I never could have done this without you. Thank you for believing in me.

# Table of Contents

# Foreword
by Max Rubin

The first time I saw Hollywood Dave Stann was at the Mohegan Sun casino in Connecticut. He was in the green room at the inaugural *World Series of Blackjack* just minutes before he was to go "on stage" and play in the biggest gambling tournament of his life.

While five other world-class blackjack players were quietly contemplating and planning their strategies, here was this punk, sporting clothes that KISS threw away for being too weird, running his hands (which happened to be in leather gloves with the fingers cut off) through his three-toned hair and yapping like a poodle bitch in heat at the dog pound. I caught his act for about two seconds and immediately thought, "OK, they brought this clown in for comedy relief."

I was right. He *was* funny (looking at least), but when the game was on, he put on his game face — which isn't that easy to do when you're a guy wearing mascara — and went into a non-stop, loud-mouth routine that had the guys in the booth laughing their asses off and the other players at the table ready to knock him out.

Before the smoke cleared, Dave had driven so many other players to distraction and had made so many clever plays that he had taken second place against the best televised field of tourney blackjack players ever — all while managing to piss off every other human in the casino. Except the producers. Dave lit up the tourney like no one else and quickly became the poster boy of the *WSOB*. In fact, GSN then hired him to deal on their *Celebrity Blackjack* show.

Since those days, over three years ago, Dave has cemented his place as one of televised gambling's top personalities and he's one of only three blackjack pros who have been chosen to be part of *Ultimate Blackjack Tour's* "Team UBT." The owners of *UBT* know that arch villains make for good TV. And they know that he's good.

The "bad boy of blackjack" can play some tourney blackjack. And he's a pretty fair hand at counting cards and liberating chips from casinos in his spare time — as evidenced by the fact that he's barred from almost every casino in Vegas (and half the ones around the globe), and not just for being rude and crude with a bad attitude.

I've come to know Dave fairly well over the past few years, and believe it or not, he's actually *not* as big an asshole in person as he is on TV. That said, he is one smart motherfucker who has analyzed the games and devised strategies that still have other players scratching their heads, and he can write and play with the best of them.

I'm saddened and somewhat embarrassed to tell you that I consider Dave a friend and there's no question in my mind that he will someday be one of the most famous and most feared (at least by anyone who's got a daughter with loose morals and bad taste) blackjack players who ever lived.

*Max Rubin*
*Fall 2006*

# VIP List

Who knew all those years ago, when I set out on this wild ride, I'd one day be staring at a completed manuscript detailing the whole damn thing? Truth be told, I've always fancied myself a bit of a writer, but I guess now it's official, huh? Weird. Well, I guess it's no stranger than setting out to be an actor, getting a theater degree, and then realizing years later that you've gone and become a professional gambler instead. Sometimes you just play the cards you're dealt. One thing's for certain, though: I wouldn't be writing these words today without the strong influence of many particularly amazing people I've come into contact with on my journey. Here's to you. Thanks for helping make this happen!

First and foremost, much love to the two that started it all: my parents. I look around in wonder sometimes and realize that this drive inside me to be the best and brightest I can possibly be, this uncompromising belief in the fact that I can accomplish anything I set my mind to, all comes from you. As a child, you empowered me to reach for the highest mountain and to never accept failure; today I feel like I'm one step closer to making all my dreams come true. I love you.

In the same vein, the constant support and care of my grandparents got me through some of the roughest years of my life. To my Nana and Nanu, thank you for always being there — and for being the first ones to bring a love of card playing into my life! More than anyone, my grandfather is probably most responsible for my future evolution into the smack-talking Hollywood Dave; he heckled me through countless rounds of Rummy as a child, beating me in game after game. And you know what? I am so grateful you never made it easy for me to win, Nanu, because when I finally learned how, I felt as if I had conquered the world. I still feel that way today. Thank you.

To Harrison, who's been a true brother to me since before I even had brothers. This is really all your fault, you know that? There I was, peacefully creating works of political theater in college with hot, angsty chicks, and you had to bring this Stanford Wong guy up to me. The first time you disappeared to Detroit for three days and lost your entire life savings playing some kind of miracle beat-the-house strategy for blackjack, I ridiculed you for weeks. Now look at what's happened. Whatever, I'm sure it's all just part of your sick plan to completely ruin the rest of my life. As if giving me that hit of LSD as a teenager wasn't bad enough. Dicksmack.

Sometimes there are those people in life you just click with right away; my renegade publisher Viktor Nacht became one of my best friends practically the day we met. Whether scheming to take down international casinos, creating a legion of New Guard gamblers (West Coast Grinders for life, yo), or just navigating the curious politics of a very paranoid underground community, Viktor is one of the most knowledgeable, talented, and hip guys I know. Together with Bettie Paige, who edited this book with the savviest of pens, they've given me the freedom (and encouragement) to create the most irreverent of blackjack works, and for that I will always be grateful.

Ah, the authors. Your words taught me the truth behind the game, and I eagerly devoured every piece of your wisdom. From Kenny Uston to Stanford Wong, Bryce Carlson to Ian Andersen, Lawrence Revere to Ed Thorp, Don Schlesinger to Peter Griffin, I am eternally indebted to you all for giving me the gift of knowledge. Props as well go out to Norm Wattenberger for giving me the expert computer training ground with which to perfect my skills!

Two authors in particular have touched my life in a personal way. Don Schlesinger has been more than generous with his time and talent in the editing of this book, as well as in opening many doors for me in the world of professional blackjack. It's not every day that an icon of the game takes such an interest in a guy who eats four-letter words for breakfast! As well, I am grateful for the constant advice of Rick "Night Train" Blaine, a man who insists on calling me his "hero" even though his own heroics have made him a true mentor to me over the years.

To Kim Holtzman, who discovered me, and Kevin Belinkoff, who created the television monster that is

Hollywood Dave: What the hell were you guys thinking?! I mean, don't get me wrong, I'm grateful, but c'mon — this *can't* be good for the world. I can promise to use my powers for good, but if I'm ever tempted to the dark side, it's officially your cross to bear! Thanks for giving me my voice and my shot at greatness.

Speaking of television, thanks to the two luminaries of blackjack TV whose footsteps I will always be following: Max Rubin and Anthony Curtis. Max, the first one in the world of professional blackjack to see through my smokescreen to the talent underneath, wrote the coolest intro to a book I could ask for — and has always been a great inspiration to me on my quest to make blackjack as entertaining as it can be. Likewise, Anthony has "been there and done that" in the world of blackjack (televised or otherwise) more so than just about anyone else, and has always been incredibly supportive of me and my growth in this industry. Thanks for opening the doors, man. Drinks are on me.

Likewise, I've been blessed with countless personal friends in the blackjack community who have become the backbone of one of the most incredible extended "families" I could ask for. If I'm a good player, it is only because I have fought to stay afloat while surrounded by so much talent. To all the fellow pros I have come in contact with over countless beers and conversation throughout the years, thank you for your insights, intelligence, and of course, for embracing my eccentric nature and making me feel welcome. We're all in this together, no matter what differences sometimes arise; at the end of the day, I've got all of your backs.

As this book goes to press, the biggest splash in the gambling world is the *Ultimate Blackjack Tour,* an exciting new look at blackjack tournaments made just for the twenty-first century, media-savvy world. Russ Hamilton, founder of the *UBT,* invited me in and has given my career as both a pro player and television personality an incredible boost. Thanks for giving me the opportunity of a lifetime.

Finally, no list of acknowledgements would be complete without thanking those who have tuned in, laughed, and learned over all the years: my FANS! You guys are the best support system a degenerate gambler like myself could ever ask for. My heart glows with every email, letter, and comment I receive, and I hope that, if nothing else, this book puts a smile on your face and some money in your pocket. In this crazy, self-serving world, it feels really good to be able to give something back to those who have given me so very much. Rock on!

*Holly Deezy*
*Spring 2007*

# Introduction

As I write these lines, a war is going on. In casinos and secret back rooms all over the world, a battle is raging between corporate bosses and a small but fierce legion of card counters and other advantage players. The turf? The game of 21, or as it's more often called: blackjack. The victims are the unsuspecting public, caught in the crosshairs. It is my self-imposed mission to educate, empower, and equip you, dear reader, with the tools you need to win this war. It is much harder to survive at table games now than it once was, as casino surveillance and deterrence methods have reduced many of my kind to a tough existence eking out a narrow advantage while hiding in the shadows for fear of discovery. The future of blackjack lies in a few surviving cash games, true, but with the unprecedented rise of poker and blackjack television coverage over the past few years, tournaments are here to stay as well. *Hollywood Blackjack* will give you a solid foundation in basic strategy, card counting, and cover play — skills you can most certainly use to gain a real edge on trips to casinos everywhere.

Lord knows there are many solid blackjack books out there already; see the reference section for a list of essential gambling books that should be in every advantage player's library. *Hollywood Blackjack* not only presents a complete system for winning at the game of 21, but strives to serve as the required primer for anyone interested in becoming a professional gambler — or just those who want to live vicariously through the eyes of the pros while picking up enough key tricks of the trade to make their next weekend excursion to a casino that much more profitable. I'll teach you to think about gambling in a whole new light and, if nothing else, entertain you along the way with a series of gambling stories yanked directly from the trenches of my personal experience — a journey that took me from small-stakes wagering in unsavory gambling halls to the final table of the *World Series of Blackjack* and beyond.

# F*&% the Stardust

"Pick up your checks, cash out, and leave. Your action's no good here anymore," said the tall, craggy, bespectacled pit boss in the Stardust's suddenly unfriendly 21 pit, with noticeable disgust in his voice. I looked blankly at him, more surprised by the old-school gangster lingo than the fact that, for the first time in my life, I was being thrown out of a Las Vegas casino for counting cards. "Your action's no good here"? "Cash in your checks"? Who talks like that, anyway?

I protested falteringly, confusedly. "Wh– what are you … I don't …" I stammered, hands outstretched (in what I perceived to be a rather reasonable manner) as if I had just been pulled over for a traffic violation and was trying not to make any sudden moves for fear of being shot in the face by some overzealous police officer. Only thing was, this was no police officer, and there was definitely nothing routine about this particular "traffic stop."

"Get out of my casino and don't ever come back," he glowered, reaching over and swiping my player's club card menacingly from the felt in front of me. Damn. I knew I shouldn't have used that. "We don't want your action around here. You're done." With that, he abruptly turned and walked toward the telephone, obviously intent on some further mischief. As if on cue, the dealer — a horrible little Asian woman with bad acne and entirely too much jewelry — ungraciously pushed my chips out of the betting circle and hugged the double deck of cards closer to her chest, to protect from what I could only guess she perceived as the psychic mind rays I apparently possessed that would compel her to deal against her own will. Her arched eyebrow seemed to silently taunt, "Yeah! What he said, punk," as if in answer to the perfectly orchestrated quizzical expression etched across my face (to be fair, I may have unjustly added the word "punk" to her otherwise crystal-clear subliminal message, but it sure seemed to apply at the time).

Right. Time to go. Nothing to do but scoop up my chips and head quickly toward the door, keeping my eyes peeled for potential stun gun attacks from over-caffeinated security personnel who would later most likely corroborate in separate incident reports how I had undoubtedly charged them with what appeared to be nothing less threatening than a machete. Of course, they were reluctantly compelled to use excessive force against me as a last resort and out of a genuine, dire concern for their safety. I quickly navigated the casino's labyrinth of slot machines and hordes of oblivious suckers — I mean, tourists — who make better roadblocks than anything ever designed by the hands of man. To this day, despite miraculous advances in human science and ingenuity (not to mention the amazing feats of intellectual prowess exhibited by the world's best professional gamblers), absolutely no logical method exists for quickly getting through a crowd of casino gawkers, and this moment was certainly and painfully no exception. Hawaiian shirts, fanny packs, and outrageous hats obscured my view, and for one horrible moment I thought I was lost.

Finally, I could see the exit in front of me, though I couldn't escape the detached, accusatory gaze of the eight billion-plus security cameras slowly panning in their smoky glass domes and tracking my every movement. My head filled with a litany of escape protocols from a dozen books I had studied on not just card counting, but more importantly, how to get away with it — with all the requisite chapters on what to do if you actually get busted. Imaginary checklists filled my head, instinctively guiding me through this inaugural escape process. Make sure you protest your innocence, but not too long or loudly: Check. Make sure you get all your chips off the table, since the casino has no right to keep money you've fairly won: Check. Make sure you do not go to the casino cage to cash in, because that's the best vantage point for security to snap the clearest picture of you: Check. Above all, make absolutely certain you do not end up in some back room or private office for a little "chat," no matter how insistent they are; it is illegal for them to detain you, despite how forcibly they would try to get you to accompany casino security to a little back room with no windows or witnesses to see the grisly details: Check?

Thankfully, it would seem a brutal "talking to" is not in my cards tonight. A few moments later, I am breathing the fresh night air on the Las Vegas Strip sidewalk, just another tourist in a city that never sleeps. Breathe. What just happened in there? My heart is racing; where did I go wrong? Part of me is swelling with pride and wearing the barring as a badge of honor; I must really be good if this big, bad casino needs to throw out li'l ol' me. I'm 150 pounds soaking wet, early 20s, and look like some punk rock experiment gone awry. To top it all off, when I got the tap, I was actually *losing* money, down a few hundred bucks from when I sat down a half hour earlier!

The real kicker is, it's not like I throw thousands of dollars around on the blackjack felt. Any good professional gambler knows that the biggest lesson of all is to never overbet your bankroll. As a starving actor playing cards to make enough money to scrape by while waiting for my proverbial "big break," creating a large bankroll was difficult. Sure, I knew enough to rob the casinos blind; but what I won in Vegas, I *spent* back in Los Angeles on "trivial" things like food, rent, car insurance (when I had it, that is), and all the essential ingredients that make up a struggling, auditioning actor: photos, résumés, classes, and the like. Being an actor is one of the few professions that demand their converts spend the *most* money in their pursuit while providing the *least* return. Ah, but the dream of success ... the joy of accomplishment once the bubble has burst ... it knows no rival. In many ways, defeating the cold and impersonal world of the entertainment industry has much in common with the allure of breaking down the glistening, ivory towers of the casinos using nothing but pure intelligence, ingenuity, and human perseverance. No, something was up. I must've been careless in some way, or just overplayed my welcome here earlier and already had some heat I didn't know about. Or maybe I had just been too cocky about my winnings — I hadn't had a losing trip in months. It had gotten to the point where I felt a little invincible about this card counting stuff, so maybe I just needed to chill out for a few hours and refocus. I'll hit the room, regroup, and. ...

Oh, shit. The room. I'm *staying* at the Stardust! Right now, a dozen security officers are probably en route to my suite to throw me out of the hotel. That sneaky pit boss has my player's club card and has almost certainly figured out that I'm a (soon to be ex-) guest. The thought of a bunch of goons ransacking my room and pulling the $10,000 in chips and cash I have stashed away there ("What do you mean, $10,000, sir? We only found $2,000. Have a pleasant drive home, and please don't let the door hit you in the ass on your way to the valet.") spurs me into action. Yeah, it's only ten grand, but it's all I have to my name. And, far from my being paranoid, there are entirely too many accounts of unscrupulous behavior by casinos when a card counter dares to take a crack at the golden egg. It makes no difference that I'm not cheating or doing anything illegal, merely using my brain to play more intelligently than most players — being discovered as a counter is tantamount to being treated like an unprotected minority before the dawn of the civil rights era. Let's not go there. Too many horror stories, none of them pleasant. The mob may be out of Vegas (for the most part), but a casino protecting its interests is a speeding freight train that your average mere mortal, present company included, just doesn't want to screw with. I break into a run as I careen toward the side entrance of the hotel, hoping like hell I can get upstairs before they do.

The elevator takes what feels like a maddening ten minutes to arrive as I try to look as inconspicuously terrified as possible. A particularly inebriated woman stumbles after her ruddy-faced husband (some awful backwoods marriage the only possible explanation for their matching gingham western-style shirts, replete with black leather string ties and cowboy boots), both of them with half-empty plastic bottles of cheap American beer in hand. Their faces betray an argument in progress, and I voyeuristically learn in no uncertain terms how displeased this gentleman's spouse is at him for not giving her more money with which to "break that there jackpot" because, clearly, the machine was about to "bust its guts."

As the elevator doors finally open, I rush in and press my floor, then huddle miserably into the back corner of the steel box as the tipsy couple loads in after me. In horror, I watch helplessly as they drunkenly press not one, not two, but *three* separate buttons on the control panel before finally getting their floor right! Visions of burly casino security guards giving my room the unwelcome-wagon treatment dance in my head as I am robbed of crucial seconds of my life, seconds that could quite possibly be worth thousands of dollars. Who appointed these idiots my own personal tormentors? Did I just die and wake up in a play by Sartre? Why does God hate me?

The three stops before my exit crawl by, but luckily the woman's haranguing finally instills an ambiance of uncomfortable, blissful silence in the small elevator. I can't help but take some small pleasure at being witness to the reality that is Vegas, the ugly truth behind the facade of postmodern glitz, glamour, and marketing. The lie we're expected to believe is that the casinos *want* us to win, that anyone can go home a Big Winner; but this contradicts the harsh reality of what actually happens when someone *does* figure out how to win: You get thrown out. *Persona non grata.* Do not pass go, do not collect $10,000.

At last, my floor. I hurriedly make my way down the dimly lit corridor, trying not to imagine the worst that could happen. I tell myself I'll probably be fine, and at long last arrive at the door to my room. Moment of truth. I stand motionless in the hallway, keycard in hand, listening intently for a moment to hear if I can discern the sounds of activity from within. Nada. No drawers being flung open, no big, hairy knuckles being cracked in anticipation of a little card-counting punk returning for a nightcap. Technically, I am not supposed to even be on the property right now and could potentially be subject to arrest, despite the ridiculousness of the situation. Realistically, I should have been read the official trespass warning downstairs if they hope to enforce some sort of legal action, but I have no doubt the pit boss and dealer will vouch for the fact that this happened regardless. The trespass warning is kinda like the Miranda warning (you know, "You have the right to remain silent, you have the right to an attorney," etc.) — something that must be read to you, but seldom actually is. At this point, I'd take an arrest over a room full of unhappy casino security officers. Deep breath ... insert keycard, and ... let's do this. Hit me with your best shot, you bastards.

Empty! Thank God. The arctic blast of the A/C smacks me in the face like an icy splash of water, sobering me for a furtive moment of clarity and control. I rush to the safe, enter the code, and — bingo! We're in business. I line my pockets with a thick wad of $100 bills and fistfuls of assorted casino chips. The Stardust chips will be difficult to cash out, but not impossible. I'll have to wait a few days, put on a disguise, and come back on a different shift, but it's not really a problem. Right now I just need to grab my clothes and get the hell out of here, which is precisely what I do. The next few moments are a blur, but I manage to get out in record time; before I know it, I'm in the elevator (thankfully unoccupied) and at last, the sweet, sweet parking lot. I laugh as I locate my car, goose pimples of relief washing over me in waves; did that really just happen? Man, I acted like a scared little bitch! I load up the car and make my escape into the calm desert night, like Robin Hood narrowly eluding the evil Sheriff of Nottingham. Robbing from the rich and giving to, well, me. And why not? Somebody's gotta take it to these bastards. It's not like I did anything wrong; last time I checked, using my brain wasn't a crime ... except maybe in Nevada. Tooling down the glorious Las Vegas Strip, breathing in great gulps of free air, I grab my cell phone and stack of casino player's club cards. Time to get another room and continue the onslaught. A line from Hunter S. Thompson's *Fear and Loathing in Las Vegas* enters my head and I laugh once again: "There's a certain bent appeal in the notion of running a savage burn on one Las Vegas hotel, and then just wheeling across town and checking into another." Oh well, you know what I always say: Screw 'em if they can't take a joke. Next!

# Thinking Like a Pro 2

First off, forget everything you "know" about luck, karma, voodoo, vibes, magic, and destiny. Cool? Here's the secret to playing blackjack or any other casino game: Everything that happens — *everything* — is just a mathematical expression of probability. That's it. The sooner you embrace that fact, the sooner you are on your way to playing like a pro. If a game has a 1% advantage over the player, you will lose exactly one dollar for every $100 you wager, over time. Sure, in the short term you'll see huge fluctuations above and below that figure — that's called "variance" or "standard deviation" — but ultimately, it's all just a mathematical construct of the game you're playing. Over a single weekend, no matter how much luck or skill is involved, your results will often vary wildly. In the long run (many weekend casino trips over an entire year, for instance), you will almost certainly be a losing player if you do not consistently apply a mathematically sound advantage.

I don't care how many crappy systems you or your friends "swear by," or how you know someone who knows someone who knows someone who "always wins" when he blah, blah, blah. ... That's all just bullshit based on nothing but short-sighted results that do not give an accurate picture of the reality I'm about to teach you. Erase those thoughts from your head before you even think about reading another word. If you don't get over those voodoo lies, you will never learn to master blackjack.

Secondly, before we go any further, you need to promise me something:  that you will permanently suspend any inklings you'll *ever* again have — now and forever — about what card you "feel" is coming next, or basing a betting decision on gut "hunches," or any other form of emotional, superstitious tomfoolery.  It ends now, understand?  The goal, from now on, is to play only *beatable* casino games, like blackjack, in which the house has a relatively low initial edge that can then be overcome by utilizing one or more advantage plays, and to do so with a studied, disciplined approach that unquestionably accepts the hard-and-fast mathematical truths governing the game.

Yes, gambling can be really fun and enjoyable — but if you don't learn to play with an edge, all you're doing is throwing your money away, and that just plain sucks.  Fun is when you *know* you're going to beat the house in the long run; fun is when you put your money on the line when you have the best of it; fun is not being a sucker for casino marketing like all the other novices who cross their fingers and toes and toss their paychecks away, blindly hoping to get "lucky" one magical day.  Fuck luck, okay?  Let other people try to harness luck — you're going to learn to harness *skill*.  It's all about the numbers, baby ... suck it up, do the math, and then comes the fun part.  But you have earn it first; you have to *want it*.  It doesn't happen overnight, but if you really stick to it, I promise you: It *will* happen.  You'll wake up one day on the other side of this training and realize all the gears have finally fallen in place, and that you've done it: You've become a professional goddamn player.

## SOME BASICS

The concept of playing blackjack with a mathematical edge was introduced to the masses in 1962, when Dr. Edward O. Thorp first published a text entitled *Beat the Dealer* that outlined how a typical casino patron could, with a little practice, play the game of 21 with a small, but realistic, edge over the casino (also known as "the house").  Prior to the publication of this book, several mathematicians had published a technical paper entitled "The Optimum Strategy in Blackjack" that outlined the first, rudimentary strategy for playing blackjack with an edge.  However, it was Thorp's refined work on these precise playing decisions based on the cards dealt that popularized what has come to be known as "basic strategy." More on that later.

More importantly, Thorp also presented the first card-counting system, which players could use to track certain cards and discern when one could push his edge even further, turn the tables on the casino, and actually "beat the dealer." Thorp's analysis of the house odds and how they could be overcome was an instant success, and the book rose to the top of the best-seller lists.

For those who came in on the short bus, let me explain some of this terminology. The "edge" is the mathematical advantage one has in a game, expressed as a percentage. Now, the house can have the edge in a game, say a 5.26% edge in the game of roulette. It can also be expressed as a negative, as in a player edge of –5.26% at the game of roulette. Below is a chart of the base house edges in various casino games.

| GAME | HOUSE ADVANTAGE |
|------|-----------------|
| Baccarat | 1.06% to 1.24% |
| Craps Pass Line | 1.41% |
| Pai Gow Poker | 1.46% |
| Let It Ride | 3.51% |
| Caribbean Stud Poker | 5.22% |
| Roulette (Double Zero) | 5.26% |
| Slots | up to 25% |
| Keno | 25% to 40% |

Interestingly enough, the games that continually prove to be most popular in U.S. casinos, slots and keno, are fueled by the largest player disadvantages. The ultimate proof of these numbers lies in the fact that the casinos consistently show a profit, year after year. Oh, they may occasionally suffer a losing day or week, but these built-in mathematical edges *guarantee* that the casino wins in the long run — just like a player who may sometimes win in the short term, but is *guaranteed* to be a long-term loser if he plays without an edge, no matter how "lucky" he foolishly thinks he may be.

The mathematical expression of edge over time is called "expected value" (EV), and is the absolute cornerstone concept in learning to think like a pro. A game such as slots, which is unbeatable, is considered to have negative EV, whereas a game like blackjack (when counting cards, for instance) can be a positive-EV game, and the bottom line difference between being just a gambler and truly becoming a professional player is that the pro plays only when there is positive EV. The first thing you're going to have to give up on your path to casino enlightenment, then, is the insane desire to play bad games. True pros react with complete disgust to games in which they know they cannot get an edge! Nobody wants to be a crazy person, right?

Gamblers make money to gamble.
## Pros gamble to make money.

Now, the edge on a game of blackjack can vary wildly from casino to casino, and even table to table, based on the number of decks in play and the rules of play. When the options available to players in a game are more generous, the house edge is lower. When the options are limited, the house edge is higher. In fact, every rule variation can be expressed in terms of the percentage effect it has on one's advantage, as you can see in the chart below. Because the percentage effect may vary based on the number of decks in play, I have listed here some of the odds just for the popular six-deck game.

| RULE | PLAYER ADVANTAGE |
|---|---|
| Early Surrender | 0.63 |
| Double Down After Splitting | 0.14 |
| Late Surrender | 0.08 |
| Resplit Aces | 0.07 |
| Double Down on 10 or 11 Only | −0.18 |
| Dealer Hits Soft 17 | −0.21 |

Looking at these numbers, you can see that a six-deck game in which late surrender and re-splitting aces are *not* allowed is 0.15% *worse* to play, odds-wise, than one in which these two options *are* permitted. Doesn't sound like a whole helluva lot, I know, but believe me — it adds up! Blackjack has the potential to be nearly a 50/50 coin flip with the house (a good blackjack game has only a 0.25% to

0.5% house advantage), whereas a game in which all the different options are taken away can easily carry a *much* higher house advantage. What card counting offers is a way to use the information in front of you (i.e., the cards being dealt out) to your mathematical — and financial — advantage.

Although card counting is the most popular method of making money in blackjack, it is not necessarily the most effective. Sloppy dealing, predictable dealer patterns, and other casino oversights that inadvertently reveal too much information to astute players, have engendered a whole new breed of pros who've developed fresh, unique ways to gain an edge over the house. We refer to this total collection of techniques that give pros a positive expectation over the house (card counting included) as "advantage plays," and those smart — and dedicated — enough to use them as "advantage players," or APs. This is a term you will hear time and again, and is your ultimate goal as you shed your former skin and remake yourself into a true professional player. APs have learned to think outside the box in their approach to playing games of "chance," and are always on the lookout for opportunities that yield a positive EV. Let's explore a few of the more prolific advantage plays used in the fight to beat casinos at their own game, presented here lovingly for your consideration.

## ADVANTAGE BLACKJACK PLAYS

### Card Counting

Card counting is perhaps the most romanticized advantage play of all. Whispered in hushed tones the world over, being an authentic card counter is tantamount to gaining membership in some nefarious secret society, like Illuminati or the Masons. However, if I had a dollar for every chump who believes he (or a friend, family member, or neighbor) is a pro card counter, I'd be a rich man! Card counting is easy enough to explain, but difficult as hell to master. It's also easy as hell to screw up. Miss one card out of the shoe, make one wrong calculation, and you could be risking hundreds of dollars on the wrong information.

Those who do invest the time and energy to truly get it down discover that, much like riding a bike, it's a skill that never really leaves you.  Becoming proficient at card counting, too, is the first step in setting yourself free from the voodoo constraints of gambling.  This is because, at its core, it teaches you how to think critically about the inherent probabilities in a deck of cards and the concept of being able to recognize exactly when you *do* and *do not* have a realistic edge in the game, and only putting your money at risk at the appropriate times.  Let's face it, people:  A deck of cards is only 52 pieces of cardboard that come up in a very finite number of ways; we're not talking rocket science here.  It's predictable, exploitable, and ultimately — profitable.

## Legality

Despite what misinformation the million-dollar marketing budgets of casinos worldwide would have you believe, using one's brain to gain an advantage over casino games is *not* a crime. As long as one is not using some sort of external device to enhance his edge (like a mirror, hidden computer, or a corrupt dealer breaking the rules of the game), card counting and other advantage plays remain very legal (and profitable) acts.

I'm not going to go into too much detail about card counting here, because most of this book breaks it all down for you in nice, easy-to-chew, bite-sized morsels, starting with the next chapter.  An interesting fact about counting, however, is that it's quickly becoming an obsolete science ... no shit!  With the current trends of casino technology, surveillance, and other countermeasures (all of which I'll discuss later) making so many advances, it's only a matter of time before card counting completely goes the way of the dinosaur.  So why teach it to you, instead of the many other advantage plays I'll mention here?  A few reasons — first, counting really is the foundation behind all advantage blackjack play, and thinking first in terms of "the count" teaches you to see the game in the right way — as a simplistic series of probabilities, with built-in advantages and disadvantages.  Second, there are still a lot of great, unprotected games out there that are susceptible to counting

— just not as plentiful as they once were. There will still be great games for years to come, and as the general public becomes more and more educated about what to look for in terms of good rules, we can only hope that the casinos will have to respond by providing better and better games (the eternal laws of supply and demand, don'tcha know). Third, the discipline required to become a professional gambler is unparalleled; you will find that this pursuit of making "easy money" playing cards is anything *but!* And as tough as it is to master card counting, the other advantage plays are even *more* unforgiving in their demands for perfect discipline — the profit margin is much higher, but then again so is the potential to lose it all. Master counting first, then you will be ready for the more advanced plays that require much more money, commitment, and professional experience to execute properly.

### Shuffle Tracking

It sounds simple enough: Watch for segments of tens and aces that inadvertently get swept into the discard tray at the same time, visually follow them through a dealer's shuffle, and then cut your clump to the top of the shoe so that you can bomb away with monster bets as soon as the game's back on — and cash in on all the 20s and 21s you hit right off the bat! This is the advantage play magic known as shuffle tracking, and its adherents swear by it. There are two components in cracking its mysteries; first, a good shuffle tracker must possess incredible visual acuity. You'll learn later in this book how to recognize clumps of cards down to the quarter-deck (for use in card-counting calculations), but shuffle trackers must be able to spot the *precise* beginning and end cards of a particularly ace/ten-rich segment — and then be able to follow those cards through sometimes complex dealer shuffles. Which brings us to the second aspect of shuffle tracking — being able to recognize exact types of shuffles employed by the house, and how those specific manipulations affect the outcome of the cards you're tracking. Just like every other aspect of casino game protection, nothing is left to chance when it comes to this. Dealers must learn a very specific "house shuffle" for each establishment in which they work, and not just use their own generic shuffle. Arnold Snyder's *Shuffle*

*Tracker's Cookbook* provides incredible insight into the exact techniques used by casinos to train their dealers and shows how, like everything else in the house that follows a rigid pattern, its secrets can be predicted — and ultimately broken — by those who know what to look for.

The biggest problem with shuffle tracking is that, unlike counting, the smallest margin of error creates disastrous effects on your bankroll. Missing the start of a segment by just a few cards — either by losing track of it as it makes its way through a shuffle, or simply by cutting the wrong part of the clump to the top of a freshly shuffled shoe — means you are launching out, unprotected, with gigantic bets into hand after hand of completely random cards, leading to big losses in the long run. The beauty of shuffle tracking, when done correctly, is that you escape suspicion from the house, because they are looking for a different pattern of behavior. They know that, in order to get an edge from traditional counting, you must first see a decent chunk of cards in order to establish your edge. Shuffle tracking can give you an edge right off the top, and as soon as it dries up, you simply flat bet out the rest of the shoe or take a bathroom break, returning for the last hand or two so you can follow the segment of tens and aces back through the shuffle and do it all over again. Genius, huh?

### Hole Carding

A funny name given to what basically amounts to exploiting a particular mistake made by sloppy dealers, hole carding happens when you are inadvertently flashed a hidden — or "hole" — card(s) in the game you're playing. The original precedent for hole carding came about when improperly trained 21 dealers would check for blackjacks (by looking under their ace or face card) in an unprotected manner that allowed observant players sitting at first or third base (the seats on either side of the table, closest to the pit) to actually see the card being peeked at. Although you can obviously imagine how huge an edge this gives a player, hole carding really came into its own when a new, mathematically perfect, set of playing decisions (an adjusted basic strategy, if you will) was developed to provide the optimal advantage in this situation, rather than just a generic edge.

Eventually, casinos caught on to this vulnerability in their games and instituted the widespread use of electronic peekers. That's the little device on the table that tells the dealer if he has a blackjack without the need to check for it by lifting the cards. Although you can still find casinos that haven't switched over to these electronic devices, the days of hole-carding blackjack have pretty much fallen by the wayside. However, the hole-carding skill is still as profitable today as it was years ago, thanks to the rise in popularity of Three Card Poker in the casinos. Since that particular game requires a dealer to manually deal himself three separate cards, all face down, it opens up the possibility for the occasional sloppy dealer to flash a hole card or two, giving players in this typically unbeatable casino game a huge edge — *if* they know what to do with the information. James Grosjean's immensely popular book, *Beyond Counting,* presents a highly mathematical analysis of several non-counting advantage plays along with the perfect system to optimally exploit those casino weaknesses, including what has become the hole-carding standard in Three Card Poker strategy.

Of course, this entire advantage play rests on the very curious assumption that an AP can plan playing sessions around very specific, vulnerable dealers who have proven to flash their hole cards with enough frequency so as to provide a reliable mathematical edge to the player. To this end, the science of hole carding is entirely dependent upon another, related, discipline: having access to accurate profiling information concerning which dealers in town have proven to be ripe for a hole-card attack! In this vein, organized teams of hole-carding APs have sprung up with the express purpose of cataloging the habits of countless dealers — not only to identify which ones flash their hole cards, but also to determine at what *frequency* this occurs. If you're sitting there right now thinking that this pursuit sounds like looking for a needle in a haystack, you're absolutely right! But where there's a will, there's a way — and, more specifically, where there's *profit,* there's an AP waiting to take advantage of it.

One such team of APs has a very fitting nickname: The Las Vegas Hole Card Mafia. Its members have the dubious distinction of having compiled an incredibly detailed database of hole-card-flashing dealers in Nevada casinos, and beyond. Sharing this information with other APs is most definitely *not* an option; not only have they gone to great lengths compiling this data, they must make sure no one inadvertently tips off the incredibly small number of dealers who fit the profile by overplaying those games. This hoarding of intelligence is a necessary team function, in order to ensure that their central management can schedule certain players on certain dealer shifts, so that the same community bankroll can profit from this advantage play without putting any one individual player at risk.

## Beyond Counting

James Grosjean's seminal work on the subject of alternative advantage plays, *Beyond Counting* has become a cult classic not only for its highly technical and frank analysis, but also because the author has yet to release a second printing of his work. Years after its first publication, rumors still abound over a second, updated edition hitting the shelves, but to this date the printing presses are still silent. This has created a very lucrative market for the limited edition of the original series, where used copies of the book sell on eBay and between private sellers for upwards of $500 a copy. The most plausible explanation for this is that he actually doesn't *want* this information circulated in such a public manner. The more information that APs print about the secrets behind beating the house, the more information we give casinos as to how they can further protect their games. This is why the *best* information on the most lucrative advantage plays will never see the light of publication, nor even discussion between rival groups of pros who must closely guard access to these secrets. A game within a game within a game — welcome to the dollhouse!

## Dealer Tells

Another nifty little advantage play involves reading dealer tells. A tell is a habit or behavior that gives the astute player more information about a hand than he would normally have from regular play. Though tells are usually associated with poker, blackjack dealers most certainly exhibit psychological tells just begging to be exploited. Tells primarily come into play during games in which the dealer must manually check to see if he has blackjack (when an ace or ten is showing). As mentioned, most casinos currently use an electronic peeking system in this situation, but occasionally you'll find a joint that still does things the old-fashioned way. Obviously, if the dealer has blackjack, he'll flip over the hole card to reveal your nemesis and scoop away your money; however, on the off chance that there's no blackjack waiting for you in the hole, watch the dealer closely as he examines the hidden card.

It may sound silly, but developing this skill can make you *beaucoup de* bucks in the long run. Often, you will be able to "read" the dealer to figure out if you are indeed up against a made hand (like a dealer 18, 19, or 20), or something in need of a little help. The best way to do this is to rely on the rapport you've hopefully established with your dealer up until this point; dealers are people, too, and generally fall into one of three categories: 1) On your side, 2) On the house's side, or 3) Couldn't give two shits about anything except Miller Time. Depending on how strongly you're vibing with your dealer, you'll be able to put him into one of these categories and use that information to discern his tells.

A dealer who genuinely sympathizes with the players will often, despite his best poker face when looking at the hole card, convey the strength of his "hand" — especially if he knows that he has your cards beat and doesn't necessarily want to take your money. The opposite is true of a dealer who seems to revel in raping your bankroll, all in the name of the almighty House; you can sometimes read the cruel delight in which he eagerly anticipates another "win" for the home team. You shouldn't deviate crazily from basic strategy until you've had a chance to observe this particular type of dealer over the course of several peek situations; you must learn to truly put yourself in your dealer's shoes, to see how he would react given his natural temperament and your relationship to him. Poker players call this "putting together a book" on someone — remembering the series of psychological traits and reactions of your opponents to specific situations. Eventually, you start to see the game through the dealer's eyes, and can guess what hand you're up against with startling accuracy. This skill takes a long time to develop, so start practicing now! Oh, and one more thing — a shortcut, if you will. Because of the index patterning of most decks of cards, a 4 in the hole is often momentarily mistaken for an ace, so very often a dealer will unconsciously do a quick double take to verify the true identity of the card. Sounds bizarre, I know, but pay attention to how often a dealer double take results in a 4 in the hole!

### Team Play

The LV Hole Card Mafia is but one of many talented AP teams operating in casinos worldwide, some as far back as the 1970s. Solid teams share a common bankroll while their members work together as an organized, disciplined force to extract as much profit as possible in as creative a manner as possible from the house. Each team prefers to use its own management style and specific money-making techniques — which can get pretty lucrative at this stage of the game (into the millions of dollars each year), as a group of players working in tandem will always be able to execute more advanced plays than any individual player could working alone. Although the mathematics behind each type of advantage play must be business-sound before putting it to use in the field, most teams prefer to isolate from other groups of APs so as to safeguard their particular "industry secrets" from overexposure. Since the very nature of being an AP involves hiding what we know from the casinos, you can imagine how protective many teams are of the hidden opportunities they exploit for profit that would immediately dry up if the casinos got wind of them.

To be honest, when I first put together my original outline for this book, there were other advantage plays I planned on discussing in this chapter — but I was ultimately convinced by some players in the AP community whose accomplishments I respect to selectively remove them.

Why? Because what would merely provide an interesting story *here* could potentially prove to ruin an incredible source of income for many teams out *there* in the real world. Some of these unique advantage plays give a team an edge of 20% or more! Which gives me an idea for an advantage play of my own: Maybe I'll consider throwing back *in* some of this sensitive information when I do a second printing of this book, unless I receive a nice little 1% taste of the action that's got so many people in a frenzy! Hey, just consider it a tribute to a fellow member of the AP community who's got your best interests at heart. ...

There have been many famous teams that have escaped obscurity to become truly notorious, like the MIT card-counting team, the Czechs, the Greeks, and the true pioneers of modern team play — Ken Uston and Tommy Hyland. One of the first well-known team plays involved the use of special counting computers (placed in a specially constructed boot or actually worn on the player's body), now illegal to use in U.S. casinos. These devices would permit an AP to play with a much higher degree of accuracy — and with all the requisite additional advantage that came with it.

Another popular play in use by many teams today involves the coordinated effort of several team members. Individual players, called "spotters," sit and play for very small stakes at different tables in a casino, waiting for the count to rise to an acceptable playing level. Then, using a prearranged signal, the spotter calls in another team member — the "big player" (BP) — who drops huge bets on the felt until the count goes bad again, at which point he is signaled out by the spotter. The BP spends the night being called in to tables with great counts, and the casino (in theory) never suspects a thing! This type of team play was first introduced by Ken Uston in his book *The Big Player*. Of course, there are always horror stories of whole teams ending up busted, but that comes with the territory. It is always more advantageous to play in an organized group of proficient APs, working off a shared bankroll that can absorb one another's bad beats. Acceptance into these clandestine organizations comes only by referral or when a new candidate is sought out through a hidden scouting process. As you can imagine, trust is the most sacred commodity a team can bet on.

## SOME OTHER ADVANTAGE PLAYS

### Video Poker

Blackjack is not the only casino game that can be beaten by APs; certain video poker machines can be exploited through a very specific set of playing decisions as well, much like the basic strategy inherent to blackjack. In the short term, the swings can be incredible — but over the long haul, positive EV is guaranteed on certain games. Not a bad way to earn a living, and many pros do. The only downside is that you must effectively trade in a sizable portion of your life to repetitively punch buttons on a machine, banging out your narrow advantage like a trained monkey. Good monkey! Does monkey wanna treat? Yum, yum! Who's a good monkey? Yes, you are ... smack the buttons faster, monkey!

### Spooking

One controversial team advantage play that can be used at a variety of card games is called "spooking," in which a fellow team member stands on the opposite end of the pit and physically watches a handheld game being dealt. From this angle, it's easier to spot the dealer's hole card and, through a series of signals, the card can be communicated to the player seated at the table. From there, the strategy involved works much like the optimal play professional hole carders use, but to be honest, this has always seemed like the one advantage play with very questionable legal and ethical considerations, so I would not recommend pursuing this technique. It's one thing to use information the dealer inadvertently flashes you during game play, but to physically use another team member as a "device" that aids in gathering the info appears to fit the legal definition of cheating. Still, many APs are known to use spooking as part of their daily arsenal when doing battle against the evil casino empire.

### Craps Sharpshooting

Sharpshooting is a theory that the human hand can be physically trained to throw dice in such a manner that controls one of three axes on which a die can spin, producing a non-random-enough result for a player to get an edge over the game of craps. After all, next to blackjack and baccarat, craps carries among the best natural casino odds, clocking in at just about 1.4% in favor of the house. Even as I write this, a fierce war rages in the advantage-player community among those who believe sharpshooting is a skill that can be developed (or even that certain players are more genetically predisposed to having this ability than others), and the majority of APs who think it's all hogwash.

For as much as this book tries to present the truth of advantage play in as accessible a manner as possible, without getting too technical, everything you read here is based 100% on the fundamental mathematical constructs that support every aspect of gambling. For this reason, I cannot personally endorse craps sharpshooting as an advantage play because, while the theory may be plausible, no conclusive mathematical evidence has ever been able to sufficiently back it up! Sure, in the short term the findings look good, but advantage play must pass the hard test of empirical, long-term results before it can be espoused as the truth. I am sure several bigwigs in the gaming industry will object to what I've just said, but that's my take on it. You heard me — no dice talk or you go to bed without any supper, understand? Good.

## THE BOTTOM LINE

Obviously, there are a multitude of ways to beat the casinos, especially at the game of blackjack, as long as you apply the right kind of intelligence, ingenuity, and resourcefulness to the equation. And best of all, you can do it *legally*. You'll notice I didn't mention anything about card bending, marking cards with infrared ink that can be seen using special contact lenses, or inside help from the casino (known as "collusion"). Everything this book teaches involves using the one inalienable object no one can ever take away: your brain. And what a marvelous machine it is! All too often the casino argument against APs is that it's "unfair" to "less-skilled" players who play blackjack without knowledge of card counting and other advantage plays. The house would rather dumb everybody down than educate the uninformed masses to play better.

So before we get to the real nitty-gritty of how to count

cards and conquer casino blackjack, I am going to ask each of you to promise me one other very important thing: Once you truly learn to think like a pro and discover the secrets of how to be a card-counting AP, you must "pay" for this gift of knowledge by going out into the world and converting three more people to the truth! Not necessarily by teaching them how to count; just by debunking their myths concerning blackjack. Tell them to buy basic strategy cards (sold in most casino gift shops) and use them at the tables. Warn them about scam games like Super Fun 21©, 6:5 blackjack payouts, and any form of blackjack using a continuous-shuffle machine. Check out Chapter 5 for a complete list of bullshit casino tactics used to screw over the unsuspecting public.

Above all, our ultimate goal as APs, beyond any sense of personal fame or fortune, should always be to stop the casinos at their own game by using the one weapon that bloodsucking beast is terrified of more than life itself: an educated public. This is now your solemn responsibility — your birthright as an AP, as it were. Before you go a step further, you must swear to spread the word, or everything you learn will eventually be meaningless and turn to dust as you yourself pound the last nail into the coffin. It is up to you to bring life back to our game, or the tombstone will forever remind us: Alas poor Blackjack, I knew her well.

Oh, wait. That's Shakespeare. Whatever. You get the point — make it right, or fuck off. Last chance to bail out; from here on in, things get intense. Put on your game face, people — it's time to crack the secrets of 21.

# So You Wanna Be a Card Counter

**Nothing** I've said so far can dissuade you, huh?
Fine, have it your way. Here it is, in a no-holds-barred
format: a complete breakdown of what it takes to make it
in the world of blackjack.

### KNOW YOUR BS!

First off, you'll need to memorize basic strategy (BS)
cold. Period. No ifs, ands, or buts about it. Basic strategy
dictates the exact decision you'll be making every single
time you're presented with a playing option. If you have a
total of 11 and the dealer is showing a 6, you will always
double down. And if your cards total 19 and the dealer has
a 4, you're going to stand. Every time. I know that a lot
of you already have a pretty decent understanding of these
things, but to be a pro you have to be 100%, even when
things get more complicated — like what to do about a soft
18 versus a dealer 3. Or a pair of 5s against a dealer 5.
And let's not forget the dastardly 16 versus a dealer ten.
Always remember: A couple of mistakes an hour may cost
you your entire advantage, so you need to be *perfect* with
this stuff. Yup. And if you're already sitting there with
a blank expression on your face because you don't know
what terms like "double down" mean — or if you don't
already have a basic understanding of the fundamentals of
how to play blackjack — then you really need to pick up a
different book or a primer on the game before you're ready
for this one.

So look, I could sit here and give you a really long mathematical explanation of *why* there is one (and only one) basic strategy play to make in any given situation, but this isn't a math-nerd book. You've got Stanford Wong for that, fuckers. But if you've got any crazy ideas about playing "hunches," or you just "feel" like a bust card is coming when you know you have to hit your 15, please refer to the previous chapter. There are NO hunches in this game of 21 — only mathematically perfect plays. That's what basic strategy is: the most mathematically perfect system of playing decisions, based on precise combinatorial analysis. I know, I know — it sucks when you have to hit a 15 just because the dealer is showing a 7. You *know* more cards will bust you than help you. You *know* there's a chance the dealer doesn't have a 10 under there. But trust me, although you may lose much of the time in this scenario by following basic strategy, you will lose *even more* of the time by *not* following basic strategy. Sometimes you just need to accept your fate. By trusting in BS, you can take comfort in the fact that you will win as much as you possibly can, without card counting. You'll just have to suck it up.

On the following page, you'll find a basic strategy chart for the popular six-deck game in which the dealer stands on a hand of soft 17. It shows the differences in play based on whether or not the game allows you to double down after you split your cards. Remember what I told you about more options being better for the player? Try to find a game that allows you to double down after a split so you can get that extra 0.14% edge. You won't find too many playable single- or double-deckers out there anymore, so this game is almost as good as it gets.

You'll notice some of the cells have two options, with one displayed as a lowercase letter, e.g., "Dh." This particular example means that you should double down, but if you can't because your hand total of 10, for instance, consists of three cards (because you already hit your hand), then you should simply hit. This will occur more frequently on your soft hands, where you would consider a hand of Ace, 2, and 4 as an Ace and a 6 for the sake of simplicity. And, I really shouldn't have to tell you that "T" stands for *all* ten-valued cards. Memorize BS, and then get back to me.

*dealer's upcard* ↓

# BASIC STRATEGY CHART

## Hard Hands

*your hand* ↑

| | 2 | 3 | 4 | 5 | 6 | 7 | 8 | 9 | T | A |
|---|---|---|---|---|---|---|---|---|---|---|
| 8 | H | H | H | H | H | H | H | H | H | H |
| 9 | H | Dh | Dh | Dh | Dh | H | H | H | H | H |
| 10 | Dh | Dh | Dh | Dh | Dh | Dh | Dh | Dh | H | H |
| 11 | Dh | Dh | Dh | Dh | Dh | Dh | Dh | Dh | Dh | H |
| 12 | H | H | S | S | S | H | H | H | H | H |
| 13 | S | S | S | S | S | H | H | H | H | H |
| 14 | S | S | S | S | S | H | H | H | H | H |
| 15 | S | S | S | S | S | H | H | H | Rh | H |
| 16 | S | S | S | S | S | H | H | Rh | Rh | Rh |
| 17 | S | S | S | S | S | S | S | S | S | S |

## Soft Hands

| | 2 | 3 | 4 | 5 | 6 | 7 | 8 | 9 | T | A |
|---|---|---|---|---|---|---|---|---|---|---|
| A,2 | H | H | H | Dh | Dh | H | H | H | H | H |
| A,3 | H | H | H | Dh | Dh | H | H | H | H | H |
| A,4 | H | H | Dh | Dh | Dh | H | H | H | H | H |
| A,5 | H | H | Dh | Dh | Dh | H | H | H | H | H |
| A,6 | H | Dh | Dh | Dh | Dh | H | H | H | H | H |
| A,7 | S | Ds | Ds | Ds | Ds | S | S | H | H | H |
| A,8 | S | S | S | S | S | S | S | S | S | S |

## Splits - Double After Split (DAS)

| | 2 | 3 | 4 | 5 | 6 | 7 | 8 | 9 | T | A |
|---|---|---|---|---|---|---|---|---|---|---|
| A,A | P | P | P | P | P | P | P | P | P | P |
| 2,2 | P | P | P | P | P | P | H | H | H | H |
| 3,3 | P | P | P | P | P | P | H | H | H | H |
| 4,4 | H | H | H | P | P | H | H | H | H | H |
| 5,5 | D | D | D | D | D | D | D | D | H | H |
| 6,6 | P | P | P | P | P | H | H | H | H | H |
| 7,7 | P | P | P | P | P | P | H | H | H | H |
| 8,8 | P | P | P | P | P | P | P | P | P | P |
| 9,9 | P | P | P | P | P | S | P | P | S | S |
| T,T | S | S | S | S | S | S | S | S | S | S |

## Splits - No DAS

| | 2 | 3 | 4 | 5 | 6 | 7 | 8 | 9 | T | A |
|---|---|---|---|---|---|---|---|---|---|---|
| A,A | P | P | P | P | P | P | P | P | P | P |
| 2,2 | H | H | P | P | P | P | H | H | H | H |
| 3,3 | H | H | P | P | P | P | H | H | H | H |
| 4,4 | H | H | H | H | H | H | H | H | H | H |
| 5,5 | D | D | D | D | D | D | D | D | H | H |
| 6,6 | H | P | P | P | P | H | H | H | H | H |
| 7,7 | P | P | P | P | P | P | H | H | H | H |
| 8,8 | P | P | P | P | P | P | P | P | P | P |
| 9,9 | P | P | P | P | P | S | P | P | S | S |
| T,T | S | S | S | S | S | S | S | S | S | S |

**H** = Hit (**h** = Hit if you cannot Double/Surrender)

**S** = Stand (**s** = Stand if you cannot Double)

**D** = Double Down          **P** = Split Pairs

**R** = Surrender

## Know Your BS?

By the way, if you really want the utmost in basic strategy information, I like Don Schlesinger's "Ultimate Blackjack Strategy Cards." Pick your poison with cards for single-, double-, and multiple-deck games, each with four charts for different rule variations. Hell, I even pimped these cards on an episode of A&E's "Caesars 24/7" once.

Anyway, you're all full of numbers now. At least some of you are, so here's your first test as a pro. No, I'm not going to give you any sort of written or memorization test — because personally, I don't really care if you've memorized basic strategy or not; it's not like *I'm* making any money off of you. But *you* should care. Don't do it for me; do it for yourself. Do it so you can increase your cool factor by a full 23% (yes, that's how much cooler you'll be once you learn perfect BS — and yes, I'd know). Do it so you can really, *truly* start on the path to taking money from the casinos — everything you do in the magical world of advantage blackjack all starts right *here*. This is the rock, the foundation that everything else is built upon. If nothing else, just do it so you're not out there screwing up at the tables while telling people Hollywood Dave taught you how to play blackjack. Don't make *me* look like an asshole for teaching you if you're not going to make it right.

Once you've done the work, ask yourself: If I were given a quiz of 100 basic strategy decisions *right now,* would I score 99% or better? Can I fill in an entire grid of BS decisions from memory? Can I do this quickly and without hesitation? If you answer no to any of these questions, you'd better stop right here before your head explodes. Oh, it will, buddy, I can assure you of that. And for crying out loud, keep your money off the tables. But *if* you're ready to move on, let's rock and roll!

## LEARNING TO COUNT CARDS

### Why Count Cards?

Okay, so you want to know the secret behind counting cards? I promise, it's not as difficult as you might think. But, like basic strategy, it is something that must be learned *to perfection* in order to work successfully. And speaking of BS, now that you've learned it cold (right?), I have some terrible news for you: Except on ridiculously rare occasions where you find a game with overly advantageous rules, playing perfect basic strategy will *not* give you an edge over the house. In a perfect world, with all the best games and rules typical of most casinos, the house still has about 0.25% on you. Yup. Which means you need a little extra oomph to gain the advantage that will give you a realistic edge — and profit — over the house.

So here's the secret to card counting: Unlike other casino games, where the next result (spin of the ball, roll of the dice, turn of the wheel) is based upon a completely random and independent event, in the game of blackjack, a deck of cards has *memory*. That is, there's a specific quantity of each type of card in a deck or shoe, and as the dealer spits out more and more cards, the composition of the remaining deck(s) changes. If you're playing a six-deck game, and four aces come out on the first hand — well, that means there are only 20 aces left, and you can take that fact to the bank. Same thing with the tens (all face cards are considered "tens") — if 30 of them come out in the first three rounds of a crowded table, then it means that there are exactly 30 *fewer* tens left. The odds of more tens being dealt out are significantly lowered, no way around it.

At a roulette wheel, even if the ball has landed on red for 20 spins in a row, the odds of it landing on red again on the next spin are still solid, at just under 50%. Math nerds call these types of games (roulette, craps, Big Six, etc.) ones that exhibit *independent* trials, versus other games (like blackjack) that are considered to exhibit *dependent* trials. Card counters have simply figured out how to exploit games with these predictable tendencies, to the chagrin of casinos worldwide.

Before you freak out and think that you have to be like Rain Man and memorize every single card that comes into play, relax. You don't. Just like BS, there are certain mathematical constructs that govern the composition of a deck of cards. So, rather than memorize every card, you just pay attention to the *surplus* or *deficit* of high cards to low cards left in the deck(s). I'll explain *how* in a minute, but first let me explain *why* this is important.

A shoe that has a greater proportion of tens and aces to non-tens and aces means that players are more likely to get 20s and 21s, and the dealer is more likely to bust when taking a hit card. In short: good for the player. Conversely, when there are a disproportionately large number of low cards left in the deck(s) — lots of 2s, 3s, 4s, etc. — then the player will end up pulling a lot of crappy hands (13s, 16s, etc.) and the dealer will bust less often when hitting. Bad for the player, right? Right.

## Uston

There are a lot of urban legends about card counting, mostly perpetrated by the movies and television. Perhaps the greatest myth of all is that it's illegal. While the casinos would like you to *believe* this is the case, there's no law (as of yet, anyway) barring you from using your brain while playing blackjack. In fact, there's actually a law in Atlantic City that makes it illegal for casinos to throw patrons out solely on the basis of skilled play; as a result, however, you will be hard-pressed to find many playable games in A.C. beyond a few eight-deck shoes with six decks dealt out. Most A.C. casinos employ a variety of frustrating countermeasures, including shuffling the cards every few hands, in order to compensate for their inability to simply throw suspected card counters out like their Las Vegas brethren are allowed to do. You can thank the late, great Ken Uston for this, as his legal battles with the state of New Jersey in the 1980s have given counters the freedom to bring their intelligence with them to the tables. A major lawsuit, fought long and hard, set the legal precedent that gives counters this "right" while in A.C.; a similar suit in Nevada, however, led to nowhere near the same results. Hey, it's tough to pass a law protecting APs in a state owned and operated by the casino industry!

So why keep count? Simple: to know how favorable or unfavorable the remaining deck(s) are to you when making betting and playing decisions. Doesn't it suck that we are asked to bet money in blackjack *before* we get our first two cards? How are we supposed to know how much to bet?! Card counting, that's how. The higher the count (the more tens and aces still available in the shoe), the more we bet. The worse the count (lots of small cards coming), the less we bet — or better yet, don't bet at all and take a quick bathroom break until the next shuffle! So when we win, we win more — and when we lose, we lose less. We put our money at risk only when we've got the best of it. Genius, huh?

### Hi-Lo, Bitches!

The next step is to establish a mathematically solid but simple way to keep an accurate count of these high and low cards as they come out of the shoe. Lots of amateur "card counters" will say they made a certain decision because they "noticed a lot of low cards coming out." Don't fall into this trap of overgeneralization. Like BS, if the count is not perfect, you are making a mistake — and every time you don't play perfectly, you are playing *badly*. Remember, two or three mistakes an hour are really all it takes to wipe out your edge in the long run! There are plenty of count systems out there, each with their own strengths and weaknesses. Some are better against single-deck games, others work better with certain rules variations, like surrender or insurance. Not to mention, some are much easier to learn and use, but sacrifice an element of accuracy in the process. A whole chapter could be devoted to the exploration of which count system you should be using for what types of games, but I'm going to pull rank here and introduce you to Hi-Lo instead.

When I was a new counter, I learned a relatively simple plus-minus system, known as Hi-Lo, that made me plenty of money. As I progressed in my training and started attacking the higher-limit games, I was ready for a more advanced system. I experimented with Lance Humble's Hi-Opt counts before finally settling on Bryce Carlson's Advanced Omega II. AOII is a level-two system (cards are assigned values up to +2 or −2, as well as the traditional +1 or −1 and

0), and is much more accurate for single-deck games and insurance calculations. It's also exponentially more difficult to learn and use, but I forced myself to adapt in order to have a greater advantage. By no means is it one of the most difficult systems: The Advanced Uston and Revere counts are ludicrously complicated multi-level systems that demand all sorts of instantaneous, moment-to-moment calculations and conversions to gain what amounts to be a very minor extra advantage over more modern systems. Fuck that, man.

And here's the rub: After a few good years with AOII, I actually *switched back* to Hi-Lo. You wanna know why? For the same reason that I'm only going to teach you the Hi-Lo count here in my book: because it's too difficult to find the kind of good games that demand the additional finesse of the more advanced systems. Why should you spend the time and energy learning a really difficult count when you'll never get a chance to flex its true power? Gone are the days of $5, single-deck, 3:2 blackjack dealt down to the last 12 cards. The best you're going to do now is to find some decent shoe games that have good rules. What's terrifying is that, with the current trends of casino greed and computer surveillance (more on all of that later in the book), it may not be long before card counting is a completely dead science altogether. Until then, it's Hi-Lo, and remember: We *must* educate the gaming public to stay away from the bad games, or one day, we will all wake up to a world of unbeatable blackjack games with 1:1 payout on blackjacks, and *then* what'll we do?! Don't laugh; that day is coming sooner than any of us thinks, and the only way to stop it is to educate the public into staying away from those games! Okay, enough ranting (for now, anyway).

Let's do this. Presented for your reading pleasure is the complete Hi-Lo count. Props go out to Stanford Wong, the Godfather of Blackjack, who popularized this very effective system, first introduced by Harvey Dubner in 1963 at the Fall Joint Computer Conference. There are even easier counts, like Knock-Out or Hi-Lo Lite, but for my money, Hi-Lo strikes the best balance between difficulty and advantage. Perfect for shoe games, this count has been the mainstay of many professional players for years. Check out the chart at the top of the next page.

| CARD | POINT VALUE |
|------|-------------|
| 2, 3, 4, 5, 6 | +1 |
| 7, 8, 9 | 0 |
| 10, J, Q, K, Ace | −1 |

Pretty self-explanatory, I know. A point value is assigned to each individual card rank. Low cards (2 through 6) are each *plus* one; the middle cards (7, 8, and 9) are considered *neutral* and are disregarded; the ten-valued cards and aces are all *minus* one. Grab a deck of cards and go through this once with me to see the magic happen: As you slowly flip through the cards one by one, add or subtract the point values in your head, keeping what's called a "running count" (RC) of the deck. For instance, if the first five cards that come out are all low cards (2s through 6s), the running count is +5. If the next two cards are ten-value cards, the running count is now +3 — because we take the +5 and adjust it by the −2, giving us a total of +3.

In this manner you can go through the entire deck, and the magic here is that the final running count number will *always* be zero (if you've done it right, that is). Yup. The Hi-Lo count is called a "balanced" count because, no matter how many decks you shuffle together, the end result (assuming you go to the very last card) will always balance back to zero, because Hi-Lo has the same number of plus-value cards as minus-value cards. Depending on the randomness of the shuffle, the running count can go astronomically high or low as you flip through the deck, but will always balance back to zero on the last card. Some other counts do not do this and are considered "unbalanced," but with Hi-Lo you will never have that inconsistency.

### From Me to You: Tips & Tricks

As you practice at home, you can test yourself by removing a card at random from the deck, counting down the deck, and then figuring out the value of the missing card based on the final running count. For example, if the count ends at −1, then obviously a low card has been removed from the deck (the last plus-value card needed to balance the deck back to zero). You can also increase the number of decks and shuffle them together, just as in a casino shoe game, and practice counting down the increased number of cards until you end up balanced at zero on the very last card. What's interesting to note about this is that, with multiple decks shuffled together, the running count has a tendency to run much higher or lower than a single deck alone, and to stay high or low for longer periods of time, since there are so many more cards to get through. Thus, the perception of a shoe being "hot" or "cold" is simply the result of a mathematically high or low count.

There are other tricks you can use to become more proficient at mastering the running count. At first, take things slow and easy — there's no need to rush through the deck(s) on any kind of speed trial. Once you feel more comfortable with counting a deck down, try this: Flip through a deck of cards *two* at a time instead of one by one. Then, instead of counting the individual cards as +1 or –1, look for opportunities to cancel out opposite pairings of cards. For instance, when a low and a high card come up simultaneously, instead of thinking "plus one, minus one," just disregard the cards altogether in the same way you would if you saw neutral cards.

In the long run, you want to minimize your mental exertion as much as possible, so any opportunity to save yourself an extraneous calculation is a good thing. It may not sound like that big of a deal, but by the time you start counting at an actual blackjack game, you'll find things so much easier if you learn to eliminate all the possible pairings of high and low cards on the table by canceling them out, rather than counting every single card you see. You'll be surprised by how very few "leftover" cards remain to be dealt with by making this simple mental adjustment to your running count. Believe me, this'll save you more than a few headaches in the long run and frees you up for all the other things you need to be concentrating on while playing.

As soon as you've become more confident with counting down a deck by flipping through two cards at a time, you can test your readiness for actual casino play conditions by pulling out random clumps of cards and scattering them on the table in front of you, and seeing how comfortable you are at quickly eliminating the neutral cards (disregarding the middle cards as well as all pairings of high and low cards), and identifying the few cards (if any) that remain to adjust the running count by.

You'll know you're ready for this final test once you are able to count down an entire deck in under 30 seconds. Don't worry if it takes you a few weeks to get to this point; the benchmark speed most pros strive for is 15 to 20 seconds (some professional players can count down a deck in just over 10 seconds), but as long as you clock in at under half a minute, you're ready to continue your training. This is unfortunately the crucial area where most recreational players skimp — and end up dumping money back to the house in the long run. Because, really, if you can't count down a deck in under 30 seconds, you will never be able to keep everything else that I'm about to teach you straight, especially since you'll be dealing with all the *other* complications of normal casino play — cocktail waitresses, smoke, crowds, conversations, and suspicious pit bosses. You've got enough stuff to worry about, and miscalculating the running count by two or three numbers can lead to disastrous problems, as you'll soon see. Other authors may kid you with promises of easier learning curves and quick riches, but I'll never be that guy. No book is going to do this work for you. Bottom line: It'll take a couple weeks of daily practice before you're keeping a running count in under 30 seconds, as well as learning to identify the remaining relevant cards to the count after mentally editing out the neutral pairs/cards from scattered clumps. Give me a holler when you're ready for the next step, okay?

## INTRODUCING YOU TO TRUE COUNT

Great, now you're a master of keeping the running count. Congratulations! That cool factor of yours just went up another full 27% and you'll now be the envy of your peer group. Seriously, dude, I wouldn't lie about that. But now comes the next grueling step in becoming the mack daddy zen sensei of blackjack: converting the running count to what's known as the "true count" (TC). This is the step that drives many people to adopt easier, less effective, unbalanced systems, but for the small inconvenience of making this conversion with Hi-Lo, you gain a ton of additional accuracy and, believe it or not, it's still a hell of a lot simpler than many advanced level-two count systems.

Bear with me for a minute here; first I'm going to

explain what it is and how to get it, then later I'll get into what you actually *do* with it once you have it. True count is important because it takes into consideration how relevant the running count is *at that particular moment*. For instance, a running count of +3 is nowhere nearly as significant at the top of the deck as it is when only a few cards remain. Because card counting gains increasing accuracy as more cards are seen, true count is an expression of the running count adjusted by the number of cards remaining in the deck or shoe. In this way, the cards are *weighted* differently depending on when they are seen. Sounds complicated, I know, but if we never adjusted the running count to the true count, we'd experience incredible bankroll swings and, more importantly, the resulting crazy bets and playing decisions would mark us as counters practically before we began playing. And that would suck.

### Getting the TC

Here's how to get the true count: Divide the current running count by the total number of *unseen* decks remaining. Yup, that's all there is to it; a pain in the ass at first, but once you get used to it, I promise it comes pretty naturally. For instance, if you're playing a six-deck shoe and the dealer's already gone through one full deck, then you divide the running count by the five unseen remaining decks to get the true count. In this situation, a running count of +10 would yield a true count of only +2 because you're dividing by the five decks left in the shoe. If, however, there were only two decks remaining unseen, the same +10 running count would be worth more, yielding a much higher true count of +5 (the +10 running count divided by the two unseen decks). Following me so far? Good; it gets more complicated from here.

In instances where there is *less* than a full deck remaining unseen — as would happen in a single-deck game, or double decker that goes past the halfway point — what you actually end up doing is *multiplying* the running count to arrive at the true count, because dividing a number by one-half (for instance) is the same as multiplying it by two. A good example would be a double-deck game halfway through its second deck, with a running count of –6. In this case, we multiply the –6 by two (again, same as dividing it by the unseen half-deck) to find that the true count is actually −12! Ouch … time for that bathroom break!

True count conversions are very important in correctly using the Hi-Lo system and must be mastered before you can take things to the next level. Unlike keeping a running count, which primarily demands a visual faculty, true count is a two-step process: visually estimating the number of unseen decks remaining, and then the mental math behind the actual conversion. Doing these sometimes complex calculations on the fly is a necessary evil of Hi-Lo, so you're just going to have to suck it up and prepare yourself to make these types of conversions on a regular basis. Six times two may be simple, but what happens when there's a +7 running count with 2 1/2 unseen decks (true count of just under +3)? It's nothing you couldn't do with a little practice, but the secret to surviving in the casinos is to look like you're not counting, of course. The *last* thing you want to do is sit there scratching your head, staring up to the heavens, adding and subtracting numbers on your fingers, and mumbling to yourself — that'll get you thrown out in a hurry! Which is the essential difficulty of card counting — it's something that anyone who truly applies himself can figure out, but to get to a point where you don't *look* like you're doing it is another thing altogether. This is where all that training come in. It's not enough to just "get it," you've gotta know this stuff so well you can do it in your sleep!

## True Count

Some pros think of this conversion as "adjusting to a single deck" rather than just dividing by the number of unseen decks. Since you *divide* when more than one unseen deck remains, yet *multiply* when there's less than a full deck left, TC conversions effectively create a single, perfect deck that inherently balances the running count with the current statistical significance of that number. If it helps you to think about it in this way, then by all means go ahead. You'll be doing an awful lot of these conversions as an AP, so it's all about the path of least resistance.

### Who Loves You: More Tips & Tricks

Some more true count wisdom for you, and then I'll tell you how you should be using this TC conversion to make money! First off, let's define some boundaries. For the sake of simplicity, you can just estimate the number of unseen decks to the closest half-deck. While you may think that the best way to estimate the total number of unseen decks is to try to look at what is left in the shoe or in the dealer's hand (in the case of single- and double-deck games), in truth the easiest way is to simply look at the discard tray. You must learn to recognize by sight how many decks are there to half-deck accuracy; it is the simplest way of doing true count conversion since the discard tray always holds the exact number of *seen* cards in the game, stacked up clearly for your estimation. In a six-deck shoe game with 2 1/2 decks in the discard tray, for instance, you automatically know there are roughly 3 1/2 *unseen* decks remaining. In a handheld, double-deck game with a half-deck in the discard tray, there are 1 1/2 decks unseen.

There's an additional bonus to using the discard tray to figure out the unseen decks: Suppose you walk up to a shoe game already in progress and you don't want to wait until the shuffle to start your running count, because the shoe's not too far along or the table conditions are perfect. You can still jump into the game; all you need to do is start the count from zero and look at the discard tray to see how many decks are now *unseen* to you. Let's say it's a giant eight-decker, and you walk up with a deck and a half in the discard tray; after playing a deck or so, the running count is +7. What would the true count be? If you answered +1, you're right: There are 5 1/2 decks left unseen in the shoe, plus the first deck and a half of the now 2 1/2 decks in the discard tray. That makes a total of seven decks that you haven't seen, and so your running count of +7 divided by seven unseen decks equals +1. Got it? Good.

It will take you another few weeks before you can confidently and quickly convert running counts to true counts without breaking a mental sweat, and it's something that no book will be able to do for you. You need to just put in the time to train and practice this skill until you feel comfortable. Unlike counting down a deck in under

30 seconds, something you can quiz yourself on relatively easily, figuring out true count certainly feels easy when practicing at home but takes on a whole new meaning when sitting in a crowded, smoky, and noisy casino! Hence, there is no particular quantifiable time frame to strive for; the best way to get ready for this is to buy several decks of casino-quality cards and spend an hour or so a day for several weeks doing this conversion.

## In Case You Were Wondering

I know some pros who have trained themselves so well that they can visually recognize the *exact* number of cards in a discard tray. No shit! Another insane skill is the ability to physically cut a deck of cards to a specific point — to the 27th card, for instance. I've never been able to do it, but I've certainly seen it done and, yes, that ability *does* impress the babes.

First, learn to estimate the number of decks remaining in a discard tray by becoming familiar with exactly what the cards look like when stacked vertically at different heights: half deck, deck and a half, three decks, four and a half decks, etc. Hardcore pros estimate by quarter-deck increments, and do all the requisite conversions this way, but for your current needs, half-decks are cool. Then go through two, four, six, and eight decks of cards while keeping the running count, stopping periodically to ask yourself what the true count is at that moment and then (most importantly) *checking yourself* to see that you've done it right. Be creative, but set a regimen of asking what the true count is at every deck, then at every half-deck, then mix it up and do it every other deck and a half. I'll be honest, this is the single most boring part of becoming a card counter, but is entirely necessary to test your ability before you set foot in the casinos. Above all, resist the temptation to play in a casino before you have this skill down cold. Until you can do it with near 100% accuracy at home, you will never be able to keep everything straight in a casino!

Oh, and one more thing — be careful not to forget the running count in the process of doing the true count conversion. It goes without saying that, once you determine the true count at that moment, you need to go *back* to the running count as more cards continue coming out. Basically, the only two times you do a true count conversion are when you're: 1) figuring out how much to bet, and 2) figuring out how to play your hand. Then you go back to the running count until the next time you need a true-count conversion. I promise you the science of card counting gets (slightly) easier from here, so if you can stick it out and master this lame-ass necessary evil, we can get to the good stuff.

## Using the TC

So now that you know how to calculate the true count, what the hell do you do with it? Pretty useless party skill for the most part, and it certainly won't help get you laid. And believe me, I know — I've tried. Here's where we put it all together, the magic that turns all the gobbledygook that you've spent months perfecting into the gold that lines your pockets. If you've come this far — and seriously put the time in to turning yourself into a trained machine bent on profit and destruction — then pat yourself on the back. The pieces are all in place, and it's time for the final synthesis. I've intentionally withheld this information thus far, until you suffered under all the discipline it took to become proficient at everything we've discussed — but now you graduate, kemosabe.

**Betting Decisions:** The primary use for card counting is that it tells us *how much* to bet, and *when*. In this way, when the count is good, we bet more (and win more frequently). When the count is bad, we bet much less (or not at all) so that we lose less. Like all things in the mathematics of counting, there are exact points to raise your bet and by how much. We're gonna go into a lot more detail on this later on in the section on bankroll requirements, but for now you can use this rule-of-thumb betting ramp chart, tailored to the particular needs of the Hi-Lo system, which will optimize your winnings while diminishing your losses:

## BETTING RAMP CHART

| TRUE COUNT | BETTING UNITS |
|:---:|:---:|
| neg/0 | 1 |
| 1 | 2 |
| 2 | 4 |
| 3 | 6 |
| 4 | 8 |
| 5 | 10 |
| 6 | 12 |
| 7 | 14 |
| 8+ | 16 |

You're asking yourself what betting units are, right? Depending on your total bankroll, you want to select a betting unit that will give you the best chance of coming out a winner without going broke in the process. If you're using $10 betting units, for instance, then two betting units would be a $20 bet, four betting units would be $40, and so forth. Again, we'll get into what kind of bankroll you'll need in the next chapter, as well as discuss more advanced bet spreads, but let's not complicate things just yet. For now, this simple chart will keep you pointed in the right direction.

A little piece of math trivia for you: Every true count increment on the betting ramp represents about 0.50% of your real, actual advantage over the house. Since the casino's natural edge generally starts at about 0.25% to 0.50% over a perfect basic-strategy player, at a +1 true count you are, basically, even with the house. +3 true count is a 1% advantage over the house, +5 true count is a 2% edge, +7 true count represents 3%, and so on. Conversely, any *negative* count translates into a *huge* disadvantage for the player, and that's why we drop down to our minimum betting unit (usually the minimum bet for the table) so that we aren't putting our money on the line when the house has a clear edge over us.

Another reason it's important to note these percentages is to realize how incredibly *small* they are. If you knew for a fact that flipping a certain coin would land on heads 3% more of the time than tails, you'd bet money on heads all day long and expect to make a killing. But the fact is, after 100 flips of the coin, the tally may very well be 40 heads and

# Martingale

Many of you have seen me play in some of the televised blackjack tournaments that dot the airwaves now, and have no doubt noticed me occasionally employing a unique kind of betting ramp called the "Martingale." This is a negative progression betting system that involves doubling the amount bet hand after hand until finally winning — a classic "double up and catch up" strategy that at first glance appears to be a pretty effective way of guaranteeing profit over the long term, but in reality is one of the fastest ways to blow your entire wad ... er, bankroll, that is. There are specific times in the short-term world of tournaments where it can be an incredibly powerful strategy, but it *never* works in a real casino cash game.

Why? Because eventually, you lose 10 or 15 hands in a row — yes, it *does* and *will* happen, regardless of how high or low the count — and you'll hit the max betting limit for the table. And then what will you do when the next step in your progression has you betting twice the max limit for the table? You can't bet enough to cover the losses, and more importantly, you repeatedly find yourself in a position to bet sometimes thousands of dollars in order to make what basically amounts to a $5 profit. Think about it: Starting with a $5 bet and doubling after every loss for ten losing hands in a row means making a $5,120 bet on your eleventh hand in order to recoup all the money you've sunk into the progression thus far. And what happens if the table max is $5,000? $2,500? *$1,000?* You're fucked, that's what. So the moral of the story is keep your arms and legs inside the ride at all times and, stay the heck away from Martingales.

60 tails; you'd have to flip that coin 100,000 times or more to start to see your tiny 3% advantage actually translate into guaranteed profit. This percentage variance decreases slowly over time and is why card counters can never be sure if they'll make money over a day, a week, or even a month. But looking at the game from "the bigger picture," you can see how *in the long run* you are guaranteed to make a profit, assuming you're able to play often enough.

**Playing Decisions:** The other key benefit to card counting — besides knowing how much to bet — is knowing when the deck composition changes enough for us to actually deviate from basic strategy. That's right, you heard it here first: Once the cards go significantly positive or negative, certain playing decisions *change* in order for you to maximize your advantage. For instance, let's say you know you're supposed to hit a hand of 12 against a dealer 2 ... but, when the count reaches a certain point, it's actually more advantageous to deviate from the normal play and *stand,* because the odds of pulling a ten are now high enough that they outweigh the normal option. So you change your strategy, to reflect the subtle changes in the underlying mathematical constructs holding the fabric of basic strategy together.

The points at which you deviate from BS for various playing decisions are called "index numbers," and there are literally *hundreds* of these index numbers, or indices, that could be memorized, which (like everything else thus far) have been determined by computers running billions of simulations in order to come up with the exact, perfect mathematical point for such harmonious fluctuations. But most of these indices will never come up in play, and as such, are pointless to learn. For example, to be mathematically perfect, you should stand on a 16 versus a dealer 7 when the true count gets to +9, rather than the normal play of hitting. But the fact is, this scenario is such a rarity that you can safely disregard this information in the pursuit of perfecting only those factors that will have the greatest effect on your bottom line. In the same way that I didn't have you spend forever learning a ridiculously difficult counting system just so you can pick up a minuscule amount of additional advantage, I'm also not going to waste your time memorizing a bunch of index numbers that will rarely, if ever, come up. And you'll be very pleasantly surprised to hear exactly how *few* indices you must commit to memory in order to complete your card counting proficiency. Trust me; have I ever led you astray?

What follows is the last piece in the card-counting puzzle, and a must in any pro's arsenal. In the mid-1980s, blackjack expert and author Don Schlesinger popularized the concept of the "Illustrious 18" — the 18 most financially beneficial indices. Even if you memorize only the first *half* of these 18 indices, you will gain 65% to 70% of the total advantage available to you by memorizing the hundreds of total possible indices, simply due to how frequently the individual situations arise. Pretty darn good, I'd say; this discovery is a serious bright spot in the otherwise completely tedious process of becoming a counter! To come this far and *not* cram these Illustrious 18 indices into your head — or at least the first half of them — is like running almost to a marathon's finish line and then stopping for a nap. Adding these to your arsenal will finally give you all the tools you need to be a feared card counter!

### ILLUSTRIOUS 18

| DECISION | INDEX | ACTION |
|----------|-------|--------|
| Insurance | +3 or above | Insure |
| 16 v. 9 | +5 or above | Stand |
| 16 v. T | 0 or above | Stand |
| 15 v. T | +4 or above | Stand |
| 13 v. 2 | −1 or below | Hit |
| 13 v. 3 | −2 or below | Hit |
| 12 v. 2 | +4 or above | Stand |
| 12 v. 3 | +2 or above | Stand |
| 12 v. 4 | 0 or below | Hit |
| 12 v. 5 | −1 or below | Hit |
| 12 v. 6 | −1 or below | Hit |
| 11 v. A | +1 or above | Double |
| T v. T | +4 or above | Double |
| T v. A | +4 or above | Double |
| 9 v. 2 | +1 or above | Double |
| 9 v. 7 | +4 or above | Double |
| T,T v. 5 | +5 or above | Split |
| T,T v. 6 | +5 or above | Split |

Note that the deviation from basic strategy occurs when the count is at the index listed and "beyond." I use "beyond" because it depends on what side of zero you're at: For positive indices, you deviate from BS at the index number and *above*, whereas for the negative indices, you deviate at the index number and *below*. Essentially, since BS decisions are geared toward a count of zero, all your deviations occur the farther you get from zero. So for the first index number (insurance), you would take insurance at a true count of +3 or higher (that's why a BS player never takes insurance, because without knowing the count you must assume you are always near zero). Conversely, when your hand total of 13 is facing a dealer 3, you would deviate from BS and hit at a TC of −2 and lower.

There are actually another four index numbers you should know for games that offer the surrender option. Again, Don Schlesinger is to thank for these indices, known as the "Fab 4." Surrender each of the holdings if the TC is equal to, or higher than, the index number.

### FAB 4

| DECISION | INDEX | ACTION |
|----------|-------|--------|
| 15 v. 9 | +2 or above | Surrender |
| 15 v. T | 0 or above | Surrender |
| 15 v. A | +2 or above | Surrender |
| 14 v. T | +3 or above | Surrender |

## A LITTLE ADVICE

The information contained in this section, while written plainly, is really the result of years of work by countless mathematicians and masters of the game. While my summary of these concepts is entirely sound, please do not be fooled by the simplicity of the language. It will take you weeks of daily study and practice to truly work this system, and three months or more to completely master it. Please do not hit the casino next weekend (or in a few months, but with only a couple of days' training) armed with this information but without the discipline to truly own it! Despite how easy you may think it is — and believe me, I firmly believe that *anybody* can get this info down with enough study — unless you can eat and sleep this material, you are not ready for the casinos.

Even when you *do* get to the point of being able to spit counting theory out in the privacy of your own home or with friends, the casino environment is completely different. Smoke, cocktail waitresses, talkative patrons, grumpy dealers, etc. — you get the picture. Don't jump in without your lifejacket — and believe me, this material *is* the lifejacket for professional counters. I've already recommended several training methods for learning the running count, the true-count conversion, recognizing stacks of cards down to the half-deck, and the like. However, the *best* advice I can give is to get yourself several decks of blue Bees (not an official endorsement, I just have a special spot in my heart for the classic, cool-ass design) and practice, practice, practice. Don't worry about buying a plastic shoe or discard tray; they're not necessary and will only slow down your training. The betting ramp should be easy enough, but make Illustrious 18 and Fab 4 flashcards to drill yourself with if you have to.

There's a resource section in the back of this book with some other helpful books and support, most notably the Casino Vérité training software, which I would recommend hands down (not an official plug; I just know it works), as well as the online community at www.AdvantagePlayer.com, where you can find all kinds of people struggling on various levels of the same righteous path as you, including many of the true masters of blackjack who are available to answer many of the unique questions you'll form on your quest to be the best you can be. Bottom line here is, it's all on you now: The section of this book on card counting is officially over and it's time to see what you're made of. Do you have what it takes to become a member of the silent army of counters, seeping into the casinos like a virus, slowly infecting the system from the inside out? Yes, you do! Make it right. Make it happen. I believe in you. And, just because I'm a good guy, at the end of this chapter is a checklist rundown of all the shit you need to know before throwing your money down on the felt, following a great story about yours truly.

## BIRTH OF A CARD COUNTER

The biggest debt I owe in my entire blackjack career isn't to Stanford Wong, Don Schlesinger, Edward Thorp, Kenny Uston, or any of the beautiful blackjack groupies that have blessed me with their own unique talents. Instead, I owe everything to a diminutive Caesars Palace 21 dealer named Danielito.

Before you rush to the tabloids with your sick and twisted thoughts, here's how it went down: Back in the day, when I was first learning to apply everything I had read in advantage play lore, I made a few exploratory trips to the Vegas Strip. I bet very small stakes, nothing that would raise any eyebrows, but I had trained as much as possible at home and was ready to experience actual casino conditions. It wasn't long before I developed a crutch for remembering the running count between hands: arranging stacks of chips to indicate how positive or negative the count was. A count of −4 meant four chips on my left, a +6 would be six chips to the right, etc. I thought I had cracked the ultimate genius method for cheating at my blackjack training — that is, until a fateful session early one morning at Caesars Palace that would forever prove to be my final exam as a card counter, and the official loss of my innocence as I entered the ranks of professional gambling.

There I was, betting my nickels and adjusting stacks of chips between rounds, when a pit boss decided to set up shop at my table and give my chip choreography a curious look. I kept cool, telling myself that there was no way he would crack my secret code, and was startled moments later when he called over another pit boss to join in the fun. To their credit, rather than getting testy, they just laughed at my antics and started making jokes about what they had obviously figured out I was doing. Still, I stubbornly refused to believe they *really* knew what was going on — besides, they weren't throwing me out, right? So I persisted, writing off their mockery and pretending to be ignorant of what they were snickering about. Then it happened — one of the pit bosses made a quick call on the pit phone (something that should've prompted an immediate evacuation from me, but hey, I was much greener then), and a few moments later there he was: Danielito.

I assumed that Danielito was a "special" dealer, sent to tables when the savvier talents of a more experienced card hurler were required. And I was right: As the pit bosses stood by and chuckled, Danielito started dealing to me — faster than I had ever been dealt to before. He tossed cards out at an incredibly rapid pace, pausing for mere seconds after I'd wave off on a hand to reveal his hole and hit cards, then scoop everything away before I had a chance to register what was going on. Faster and faster he dealt, and in the whir of flashing cards and flying chips, I simply had no time to adjust my chip stacks for the count. The pit bosses laughed as I made futile attempts to keep up with the count, but before I could move my chips, Danielito was pitching me more cards; he was too good, too fast, I could feel the blood rising to my face ... and then it happened. Just when I thought the jig was up, that I couldn't possibly keep up, and with the chip stack crutches I had so relied on now lying in a useless, jumbled pile in front of me, it all came crashing down and in a moment of pure focus, I realized for the first time the most amazing thing of all: *I didn't need the chips to help me keep count anymore.*

It was all there in my head, clicking and whirring away like clockwork — the running count, the true count conversion, the right betting ramp and Illustrious 18 indices — everything. I would never forget this moment. I looked up at Danielito and the pit bosses and I *laughed* — because there, in the belly of the beast, at that exact moment in time, a card counter was born. And I had a casino to thank for it, forever catalyzing that violent synthesis of knowledge and passion, discipline and pure gonzo ambition to beat the house at its own game. You see, despite everything I rail against, in my heart and soul I really do owe it all to the house — the system that created me and now tries to destroy me, that which spawned me and now spurns me. But deep down I know that it is a debt I can never repay. It is at once my genesis, my catharsis, and my ultimate undoing. And it's all because of you, Danielito.

# CARD COUNTING CHECKLIST

I. Learn basic strategy
   A. Memorize the BS chart
   B. Quiz yourself constantly
II. Learn Hi-Lo
   A. Keep the running count
      1. Cancel out neutral cards and high/low pairs
      2. Count entire table at once in a face-up game
   B. Convert to true count
      1. Calculate unseen decks using discard tray
      2. Divide RC by unseen decks
   C. Use TC for betting and playing decisions
      1. Optimize winnings with the betting ramp chart
      2. Use Illustrious 18 and Fab 4 index numbers
III. Don't Be a Jackass
   A. Practice until everything becomes instinct
      1. Daily practice is essential
      2. Practice with distractions
   B. Brush up on skills before each casino trip
      1. Basic strategy quiz
      2. Deck estimation
      3. TC math
      4. Index number tests

# Doing It Like a Pro

**There** are a lot of factors to consider when deciding what table to sit down at before laying conquest to the green felts of your local casino. In a perfect world, you would be left alone to play heads-up against a dealer at 200 hands an hour, with no annoying heat from pit bosses or interruptions by prostitutes. The decks would be dealt all the way to the bottom and the rules would be more than generous. Alas, that's seldom the case and, unfortunately, choosing the best table to play often involves selecting the lesser of a myriad of evils. Here are the most important criteria to use in determining whether a game is a gold mine or highway robbery.

## RULES

By far, the rules are the most important factor in game selection. This includes whether the dealer hits or stands on a soft 17, what types of hands can be doubled, if surrender is available, blackjack payouts, etc. RUN, don't walk, from a table where blackjacks pay even money or the dreaded 6:5 scam! Remember the chart in Chapter 2 of rules and their effect on your starting advantage? Here are a few more nasty ones, more commonly found at single-deck games:

| RULE | PLAYER ADVANTAGE |
|------|------------------|
| Double Down on 11 Only | −0.64 |
| Blackjack Pays 6:5 | −1.70 |
| Blackjack Pays Even Money | −2.26 |

Notice just how nasty the newly popular 6:5 payout is on your edge — the best card counter in the world couldn't overcome that kind of house edge. It's an unfortunate fact that casinos market this as a *good* rule for the player; it's an even more unfortunate fact that there are plenty of idiots out there who believe it. Just because the numbers are bigger, they think they're getting more money. Well, *someone* is, but you can bet it's not the players!

Obviously, then, you would want to sit down at a table where the dealer stands on a soft 17, that allows surrender, doubling after a split, resplitting aces, and offers a full 3:2 payout on blackjacks (mandatory). While single- and double-deck games are preferable to a shoe game, there simply aren't many of those games left with playable rules, so finding a shoe game with decent rules is imperative. Before walking into a casino, you should be aware of the effect these rules variations have on your advantage so that you are not *taken* advantage of. The greedy bastard casinos will do anything to increase their bottom line.

This is why it's so important for us as players to collectively bar ourselves from casinos that employ shady marketing practices, such as the promotion of 6:5 payouts, and then try to cover up this incredible scam by promoting the fact that the crappy games in question are, after all, single deck. Who cares? They take away nearly 2% of my edge by offering crappy rules, and then give me a half-percent back (the difference in player advantage when playing a single-deck game versus a shoe) and expect me to be grateful? Screw that!

## PENETRATION

Hey, stop snickering! After the rules, this is what makes or breaks a good game. Simply put, penetration (or "pen") is how deep into a deck or shoe the dealer will deal before shuffling. It's often expressed in terms of a percentage, where 0% is not dealing at all and 100% is dealing all the way through to the very last card. Dealing 26 cards of a single-deck game or three decks of a six-deck shoe is expressed as 50% penetration, for instance. Dealing roughly 1 1/2 decks of a double-deck game or about six decks of an eight-deck shoe would put the penetration at about 75%, depending on exactly how many cards are dealt before the shuffle. You already know that the count becomes much more significant as more cards are seen, so the deeper the pen, the more your AP "powers" grow.

As you can imagine, casinos offer better pen when more decks are in play. Because merely increasing the number of decks in play decreases the player's advantage, the casinos feel that they are "safe" offering better pen at games with a naturally higher house advantage. For example, 80% penetration at a six-deck shoe is definitely available at many casinos, whereas you'd be hard-pressed to find a single-deck game dealt anywhere near as deeply as that. It's crucial to play at tables that offer the best balance between deep penetration and favorable rules. Now you can appreciate why the bastard casino bosses offer *better* rules at *crappier* games. Eight-deck shoe with 70% pen? No problem, do whatever you want, short of setting the table on fire! Oops — now you want to sit down at a double-deck game with 80% pen? We'll just take back your ability to surrender, resplit aces, double after a split, and oh yeah, how about a nice, whopping 6:5 payout on those blackjacks while we're at it?!

## CROWD

Crowd refers to how many people are going to get between you and the dealer. In this case, two's company and three's *definitely* a crowd. Ideally, you'd like to be one-on-one with your enemy — I mean, the dealer — so that you can not only play the maximum hands per hour (about 200 if you're lucky), but also so that *you alone* share in the rewards of your counting efforts. There's nothing worse than waiting out a few cold decks, finally seeing the count skyrocket, and then watching helplessly as your max bet is met with a 16 while the other three idiots at the table all end up with 20s and 21s! You feel like *they're* profiting from all *your* hard work. Fuck that, dude.

It's always better to find an empty (or nearly empty) table for the optimal playing experience. But one caveat: Like the correlation between finding better rules at worse games, there's also a connection between the amount of heat and scrutiny you will receive at a full table versus one where you are playing alone. Watch how quickly the pit boss plants himself at your table and starts sweating your action when the casino's empty and, conversely, how many crazy plays and what kind of wild bet spreads you can get away with while blending in with a sea of people. You need to be aware of these factors when selecting a game, and find the right balance. Definitely don't shy away from the heads-up games, but know that you will have to employ much more sophisticated camouflage plays (discussed later) as a result.

Another thing — in terms of crowd, it really doesn't matter if the other players at the table are fellow pros or hopeless ploppies (a snide term some of us elitist smartypants counters use to refer to the 99.9% of casino patrons who play without any edge whatsoever). Generally speaking, however, pros will avoid sitting at the same table as one another out of professional courtesy — and will, in fact, refrain from talking to or acknowledging one another's presence at all (more out of shared paranoia than anything else!), and you should give the same respect as you can rightfully expect to receive. Of course, this also means that you are completely within rights to chase another AP off your table if he fails to give you this courtesy. Watch how quickly he vanishes into the night after you loudly proclaim something along the lines of, "Hey, you're that guy I saw on TV talking about counting cards, aren't you?!"

## LIMITS

Limits refers to how much money the casino will let you put into action on the felt. $5 and $10 tables are common, as are $25 and $100 tables, but they come in all sizes. Some casinos offer blackjack for two bucks, others reserve private tables in posh salons for guests wagering $1,000 or more per hand. You should know *before* you walk into a casino what your preferred limit is, dependent upon your available bankroll. There are mathematical formulas that exist to determine what limits you should stick to in order to have the best chance of making money without busting out over the long run, and I discuss some of them next. Additionally, most tables have a maximum bet limit in addition to their minimum, which is not as important unless it is unusually low. Generally speaking, the maximum bet should be at least 20 times the minimum bet, which will give you plenty of room for profit.

## MONEY MANAGEMENT

Making money at blackjack is not a straight upward climb, but rather a drunken, stumbling man's pace slowly uphill. There will be many setbacks and pitfalls along the way, so the key to consistently making money in the long run is to plan for these swings and practice a vigilant and disciplined money management system that takes into consideration the inherent risks of gambling. This means finding an acceptable level of personal financial risk based on the hard facts that correlate to three key factors: your total available bankroll, the stakes being played, and the bet spread you are using (specifically, the maximum bet you are prepared to use in the highest of counts). If you have only $500 to your name, you would be foolish to put it all out on one single bet; conversely, with a $50,000 bankroll you no longer need to play at the $5 tables. But somewhere between these two extremes lie an optimal bankroll and bet size.

Despite my presenting this material after the other topics, money management is probably the most important concept in becoming a professional AP, aside from the actual counting skills. It's also a concept that is unfortunately overlooked by many amateurs trying to turn pro — often with disastrous financial results. In the last chapter, during the section on using the true count and the betting ramp chart to determine how many units to bet per hand, I mentioned I would discuss later more advanced betting spreads and how to figure out what kind of bankroll you need for what types of games. Well, that time is now, so strap on your thinking cap.

### Accepting Variance

No matter how good a player you are, how well you memorize basic strategy and counting theory, or how positive the count gets during game play, you will experience incredible financial swings. This is called "variance" or "standard deviation," and can lead to some really staggering fluctuations, both up and down, of your bankroll. Most recreational players refer to this natural ebb and flow of variance by using terms like luck, hot streak, cold shoe, hot dealer, cold cards, playing the rush, etc. — but I assure you, there is *nothing* special about these types of extended winning and losing streaks. They are mathematically built in to the blackjack equation and, far from being unexpected, are absolutely guaranteed to make an appearance in practically every session you play. You *must* be prepared for this eventuality, because to not do so spells certain doom for your bankroll. There are times when you will lose ten or more hands in a row, no matter how astronomically high the count is — as well as times when very negative counts demand the placement of nothing but minimum bets, despite inexplicably receiving blackjack after blackjack from the dealer.

I have watched in horror too many times as a week's worth of gains evaporate in a few scant moments; in fact, I once lost the profit from an entire six months' worth of playing in one cursed, 48-hour trip from hell, in which it seemed the dealer would hit to 21 every single time I had a max bet out and a 20 for a starting hand. But rather than blaming bad luck or falling prey to a victim-like mentality, you need to remember that these situations not only *can* occur, but they most certainly *will*. Even though you know you have an advantage in the long run, I promise there will be plenty of moments in the short term that will make you want to go out and put a bullet in your head, moments that will shake the very fabric of your belief in the mathematics of card counting and advantage play. You can only stop, reevaluate your play to make sure you are still putting your money out at the right time and making the right decisions, and recognize that this is all part of the sometimes torturous "fun" of 21.

## Bankroll and Risk of Ruin

Part of playing like a pro lies in never overbetting your bankroll, but unlike the hard-and-fast math that governs other aspects of the game, bankroll and bet sizing involve a subjective quality: the level of risk you are personally willing to accept concerning your money. Figuring out one's risk of ruin (RoR) — the chance of losing your entire bankroll given certain betting patterns — is an obsessive practice of professional gamblers who have learned to look at their play as a financial investment. As with everything else in the world of blackjack, there is a mathematical formula by which we can determine the answers.

Accepting a high RoR, for instance, means you're betting a higher percentage of your bankroll at any given moment, but have a comparatively higher EV ("expected value," the return on your initial investment) and must also embrace much higher variance. Choosing to have a lower tolerance for RoR means that you are betting a much smaller fraction of your total bankroll at any given point, which keeps your variance down but also means your EV is lower, and therefore your play does not yield the same profit. In this way, you must make the subjective decision about how much risk you are prepared to accept concerning your bankroll. A higher RoR equals higher EV and potentially more profit, but also a higher chance of going broke, due to the increased variance, in the process.

## Going Broke

Losing your entire bankroll may certainly suck, but it can be a great way to get outta speeding tickets! As I went tear-assing outta Vegas at 100 m.p.h. one night — after a horrifying 48-hour series of sessions from hell — a state trooper pulled me over and proceeded to do the whole "license and registration" thing. Needless to say, I was completely at my wits' end, and I frantically apologized while crazily emphasizing the fact that his town had just taken every penny in my life and I had no clue how I was gonna buy food tomorrow, much less pay any of my bills, and that I would most likely be homeless by the end of the week. My sheer manic terror worked; obviously, this was not the first time he had heard this sad story. So, what'd he do? Let me off with a warning — and made me promise to come back to visit real soon.

Several methods exist to figure out your exact RoR in any given situation, but the conservative rule of thumb is to make sure your total bankroll is one hundred times your max bet. Ready for me to blow your mind? That means if you're playing with a 1 to 8 bet spread (betting from 1 unit to 8 units at the highest counts) — where your single unit bet is the table minimum and your max bet is eight times the table minimum — a $5 table would demand a starting bankroll of no less than four grand ($5 minimum = max bet of $40, multiplied by 100 = $4k). Yikes! How many times have you sat at a $25 table with a few hundred bucks in your pocket and tried to "get lucky"? We've all done it, but a quick look at this RoR calculation and you can see how much incredible risk you take on with that strategy.

Of course, at least 100 times max bet is a pretty conservative RoR that virtually guarantees you never go broke, but believe it or not, it is probably one of the smartest and most common practices of professional gamblers. The curse is that it's much harder for a beginning pro to build up the kind of bankroll that allows for a conservative RoR with any meaningful EV. The age-old adage still applies: It takes money to make money. The problem with pushing RoR too high, as many pro gamblers just starting out are forced to do when playing on initially limited bankrolls, is that eventually you will hit a losing session and, rather than taking just a small hit, it will wipe out your entire bankroll. Then you have to start all over again, usually with an even smaller bankroll and even higher RoR — which results in another inevitable wipeout. This is why so many small-time gamblers never break through to the big game; they are constantly in a state of flux, starting from scratch over and again. It's always better to grow your bankroll at a slower, safer pace than to accept too high a RoR and lose it all. It sucks, I know, but I'm just trying to be honest here.

So what kind of a responsible money management strategy will allow your bankrolls to grow with an acceptable RoR? Well, ideally you should have access to a solid $4,000 starting bankroll that will free you to play the $5 tables with no immediate risk to your bottom line. And before I go any further, let me define what I mean by bankroll: This is money you have freely available to devote to gambling and only gambling; if you are playing with next month's rent or your mom's bail money, you already know you're screwed and don't need me to tell you that. Using the same resources to gamble with as you do to pay your bills is only asking for trouble; that effectively turns every car payment you make into an additional session loss that demands even higher profits to compensate. Remember, you're playing with only a 1% to 1.5% advantage here; you'd be surprised what an incredible *disadvantage* a couple hundred bucks a month in porn rentals can be to your bankroll.

Trust me, I should know: I originally turned to blackjack advantage play as a means to survive while a starving actor in L.A., so of course I was not only playing with my rent money but actively pushing my RoR higher and higher to compensate for the diminishing bankroll. And of course, I got cracked several times and had to come back from Vegas with my tail between my legs, borrow money from a compassionate girlfriend, sympathetic friends, and other true believers and start all over again. Eventually, I learned correct money management strategy and was able to build my bankroll up to a point where I could play without too much RoR. Going broke all the time is no fun at all, and it's enough to drive anyone to drink. Which (despite popular opinion) never really solves any problems anyway, no matter how many answers you may think are at the bottom of that bottle. Ah, liquid courage. ...

If an initial bankroll of $4,000 is a problem, then you need to look at other alternatives. No, I don't mean robbing an old lady for her social security check. One of the easiest adjustments you can make without too much trouble is to decrease your betting requirements to the point of making your bankroll 50 times your max bet rather than 100. This cuts your opening bankroll to $2,000 for a $5 table with a 1–8 bet ramp spread, and does not push RoR too high (though, to be fair, it is *exponentially* higher rather than just twice as risky), but is the absolute farthest I'd recommend pushing your RoR without being a dick about it.

So now that your minimum bankroll requirements are all figured out, you need to ask yourself the *real* question: How much money do you need to make *per hour* for card counting to be a worthwhile investment of your time and energy? It's easy to do EV calculations — just assume you'll make 1.0% (a generous average) of the total action you put on a table per hour to see your new "hourly wage." For instance, if you are starting out with a $4,000 bankroll playing at a nickel table with an average bet of $10 and assume an average of 80 hands an hour, you're putting out about $800 in total hourly action, 1.0% of which is only $8.00. That's right, you read it here first: Eight measly fucking dollars an hour. Glamorous, isn't it? Now, if the count goes astronomical, or you jump in and out of tables at higher counts, or increase your variance and play with bigger betting units at a lower bet ramp — you can double or triple this hourly figure. But still, the point is made; perhaps a better question than "How much bankroll do I need to play?" would be "How much do I need to make an hour to justify turning my life as I know it over to the great blackjack gods?" Working backwards like this makes a lot more sense, especially since it quells the temptation to overbet your bankroll and end up broke and homeless, with nothing but a sad, sad story to tell.

### Bet Sizing

One way to get greater mileage out of smaller bankrolls is by limiting your bet spread. Remember the Betting Ramp Chart on page 39? It shows a maximum bet of 16 units (at a +8 count and higher), which is an optimal range for profit. However, when playing on a smaller bankroll (or in conditions where you're dealing with above-average casino scrutiny, discussed later), you can reduce this spread to 1–12 (hitting your max bet at a TC of +6 and above), 1–8 (max bet at +4 and higher), even all the way down to 1–4 in the most extreme of conditions (maxing out your top bet at TC of +2). You don't really wanna go lower than that, because 1–4 is generally considered to be just above the breakeven point in terms of gaining enough profit (positive EV) to offset the negative swings over the long haul (negative EV). Conversely, with a larger bankroll, you can push your bet spread to 1–20 or higher — as long as you can get away with it, that is!

Another way to get more bang for your buck is to play two separate hands at once, which increases variance as well as potential heat from surveillance and the pit critters. It's also a good way to respect the RoR limits of a smaller bankroll while maintaining higher EV. While playing two hands at a 1–4 bet spread, for instance, your 50 times max bet bankroll can be even smaller — in the case of a $5 table, you're now down to just a $1,000 starting bankroll. Much less than that and you're just asking for trouble, sooner or later. There are other considerations to factor in when it comes to adjusting your bet spread from 1–4 to 1–20 and back, most notably the amount of heat you receive from surveillance, but I'll cover that later in the section on camouflage. It's always better to use as large a spread as possible, but to do so you must be adequately bankrolled, and right now we're primarily concerned with the effects bet spread has on RoR. It's hard to get rich if you go broke in the process, right? One of the best ways I know to get screwed as a pro player (outside of a daytrip to the Bunny Ranch) is to overbet your bankroll.

There is a lot more detailed mathematical information available on tinkering with the exact formulas of bet sizing and risk management; we could devote an entire book to discussing how to calibrate a very specific RoR for every type of bankroll, table stakes, and bet spreads down to the actual percentage chance of doubling a bankroll versus completely busting out. For instance, many pros like to set their RoR at no higher than 3%, but the time it would take to delve into all of the math behind such calculations would not necessarily provide answers that deviate significantly from the rules of thumb already listed here.

If you really wanna be a propellor-head geek, by all means check the resource section in the back for other important blackjack reference books to read up on RoR calculations and more importantly, the Kelly Criterion — a type of betting that theoretically never leaves you broke, as you bet only a percentage of your bankroll that correlates to the percentage of your actual edge over the house at that time. But, much like the reasons I taught you Hi-Lo instead of a more advanced count, and had you memorize only the Illustrious 18 and Fab 4 rather than dozens (or hundreds) of other indices, the time I could spend on advanced betting techniques would be much better served elsewhere. There is tons of other material to cover and I swear I've got adult ADD, so presented here for your pleasure is a simplified chart of practical, cut-and-dried, advice on bankroll requirements for various betting units and bet spreads.

# BANKROLL CHART

*bet spread* ↘ Minimum Bankroll in Thousands of Dollars

*betting unit* ↗

|         | 1–4       | 1–8        | 1–12        | 1–16        | 1–20         |
|---------|-----------|------------|-------------|-------------|--------------|
| **$5**  | $1/$2     | $2/$4      | $3/$6       | $4/$8       | $5/$10       |
| **$10** | $2/$4     | $4/$8      | $6/$12      | $8/$16      | $10/$20      |
| **$25** | $5/$10    | $10/$20    | $15/$30     | $20/$40     | $25/$50      |
| **$50** | $10/$20   | $20/$40    | $30/$60     | $40/$80     | $50/$100     |
| **$100**| $20/$40   | $40/$80    | $60/$120    | $80/$160    | $100/$200    |
| **$200**| $40/$80   | $80/$160   | $120/$240   | $160/$320   | $200/$400    |

Along the left-hand side of the chart above are several common betting units, and along the top of the chart are various common bet spreads. Where your desired betting unit and bet spread intersect in the chart is the amount of money you should have set aside for your bankroll, displayed as 50 and 100 max bets, in *thousands* of dollars. The first number in each column represents the minimum bankroll for 50 max bets when playing at that corresponding bet spread and betting unit; the second number is for a more conservative 100 max bets. These recommendations should be considered the *bare minimums* for each; of course, the choice to accept the slightly higher RoR with a 50 max bet bankroll as opposed to a full 100 bets is entirely up to you. Obviously, the higher your RoR, the higher your EV, but along with that comes increased variance and, of course, an increased chance of completely crapping out and having to start all over again from scratch with a brand-new bankroll. Which, as we covered before, really sucks.

Only *you* can decide what level of risk is appropriate given your life situation, responsibilities, and the like. If you attempt to play with less than the minimum bankroll listed, you're just asking for trouble. Personally, I wouldn't dream of playing with a bankroll of anything less than 100 times my max bet with at least a 1–8 spread, but hey, that's just me. *Caveat Emptor,* baby: Let the gambler beware!

# ·5·

# Blackjack Is Dead

**Before** I can let you loose to embark on your journey into the realm of all things blackjack — and your path to becoming a truly profitable player — I've gotta bring you up to speed on the current state of affairs in the wonderful, wacky world of advantage blackjack. Unfortunately, the sad truth is this: Corporate greed has killed the game.

The entire gaming industry thrives on a state of constant paranoia, wanting their patrons to have just enough knowledge about the games they play to *feel* as if they're playing with an edge (because gamblers who perceive that they cannot win will stop playing sooner than those who think they have a "secret" winning system), but not too much information, because then they might *actually* win. It is a high-wire balancing act, and the essential paradox of the relationship that exists between casinos and many gambling authors. If you want to be a hotshot at the game of 21, you're going to have to familiarize yourself with all the pitfalls and roadblocks that are waiting for you out there in Casinoland before they can be overcome. As the saying goes, "before we can conquer the enemy, we must first understand him."

## GAME VARIATIONS

After Dr. Thorp's book *Beat the Dealer*, which outlined how a typical casino patron could play blackjack with an edge over the casino, was published and became a national bestseller, the casinos were terrified. They envisioned an army of card counters descending upon their apparently now-vulnerable blackjack games and driving their empires into unexpected bankruptcy. In a panic, casinos all over Las Vegas started to change their house rules for blackjack, severely limiting when and how players could split and double down their cards, in an effort to increase their house edge and make it harder for the player to overcome the odds. When this happened, casino patrons revolted and stopped coming out to play these unfair blackjack games in droves, and rightly so.

Amazingly, the vast majority of these angry players were *non*-counters. No one likes to play a game that *feels* unbeatable (even if it *is,* as in the case of most casino games), and after only a few weeks, the casinos realized that *actual* revenue losses due to a multitude of unhappy customers who would not play their games far outweighed any imagined *potential* losses they might suffer at the hands of a few skilled card counters. So, as quickly as they were instated, these drastic rule limitations were reversed, and normal blackjack play was once again restored. Imagine the surprise when the casinos actually saw the profits in their coffers *increase* after only a few short months! How could this be, with Thorp's book selling so many copies and more people than ever gambling that they, too, could beat the casinos at their own game? The answer is an important one if you are to become a true advantage player: Most people who study card counting only *think* they have become card counters.

The truth is, most people read a few chapters of a book that promises to quickly and easily teach them how to be big winners, do a few quick exercises at home (or even worse, on the plane en route to Atlantic City), and convince themselves that simply because they have understood what they've read, they now have enough knowledge to make a killing at the tables. I refuse to stand idly by and allow that to happen to the readers of *this* book; you can't deny that I *never* said it would be easy, and that I entreated you to study and practice *every* step of the way. The road to becoming a profitable player is long and hard, but entirely attainable for anyone dedicated to the craft.

The biggest problem you'll face as a player is finding blackjack games with a house edge that can be overcome by counting. This is because the casinos have, once again, dedicated themselves to changing the structure of blackjack in such a way as to unfairly tip the balance of power sharply back into the house's favor. The question as to why the general public is not responding the way it once did, staying away from blackjack tables en masse and forcing another reversal, can be answered simply: *This* time, the changes to the game are much more subtle than they were years ago.

Believe it or not, casino profits increase steadily year after year, with few exceptions. And, even though the casinos are now reaping the highest percentage advantage they've ever had at blackjack, the gaming public is largely unaware of it, due to a basic lack of understanding of how these subtle changes actually affect the fairness of the game. You have to give the crafty casinos credit for this great rock-and-roll swindle; whereas in the past, their additional advantage was derived solely by taking away players' options, their extra edge is now derived by a combination of adding many creative rules for the player, while also taking away a single, overriding one.

For example, you can now find many bastardized versions of blackjack that look very appealing at first glance, but in reality are sucker bets. Super Fun 21© and No-Bust Blackjack are the most widely available of such scams currently being perpetrated by casinos on an unsuspecting public. These games offer bonus features that the general public finds "fun," such as the player wins against dealer ties, doubling down on any three cards allowed, and automatic wins for un-busted five-card hands. However, the games also remove the full 3:2 payout on blackjacks, which more than negates any actual advantage gained by the addition of these "cool" new rules, especially when coupled with a small per-hand fee (common in California and some Indian casinos).

They've accomplished this through the clever use of techniques designed solely to limit an *uninformed* player's potential advantage over the house. To avoid player backlash, casino marketing departments spend exorbitant sums of money to market the horrible games in such a flattering light that the public's overall perception is that Super Fun 21, No-Bust Blackjack, and reduced blackjack payouts are actually *better* to play than "regular" blackjack. Truth in advertising, my ass!

## TABLE MANAGEMENT SYSTEMS

Even with their obvious and ever-growing house advantage, the sad truth is that casinos spend ridiculous sums of money annually on anti-card-counter surveillance and other methods of counter discouragement that rival even that of the CIA. Don't laugh; some of the programs in use are the same ones developed to catch terrorists and other criminals — no shit! Facial recognition systems and other high-tech identification devices exist alongside computer programs that monitor games in progress to determine if anyone's betting or playing decisions correlate with one of dozens of count systems. While most monitoring devices are used behind the scenes by the surveillance departments, one of the most nefarious of these is used right on the casino floor, and it's called TMS.21™.

Never heard of it? It's more commonly referred to by its original name of MindPlay, but its official name is TMS, which stands for Table Management Systems. TMS.21 is an electronic system, built directly into the blackjack table, that literally keeps track of every card in play in the order that it comes out of the shoe. Invisible-ink barcodes are printed onto the side of each card, and the system reads the stack of cards and knows when the cards are being dealt out, and which card goes to which player. It also accounts for all the bets made by the players at the table through a dealer input screen or — get this — special chips that are outfitted with tiny radio-frequency transmitters. Computers embedded under each table read the chip and record how much each player is betting.

The system is used to thwart card counters by relaying all of this information to the pit, which keeps watch over the tables via a computer screen. Some of the information that it relays includes the count of the deck, allowing the dealer to shuffle whenever the deck becomes more advantageous to the players than it is to the house. This is called "preferential shuffling," and is a common tactic used by casinos to discourage counters. TMS.21 is also capable of notifying surveillance personnel when it recognizes certain betting patterns that correlate to the count and mark a player as a counter. Although it is illegal in the U.S. for players to use electronic devices to aid in determining the outcome of a game, this doesn't stop casinos from doing *the same damn thing* to its customers to get an unfair edge of their very own!

The insult doesn't end there: The official public relations cover story is that the system is used merely as a means to more accurately ascertain how many comps players have earned as a result of their play. Comps! Casinos argue that the "old-fashioned" method of estimating a player's complimentary dollars by correlating the hours of play and average bet with the game's edge is just not reliable enough for their valuable customers. Another excuse they use is that high-end players are getting more comps and the lower players less, simply because the high-end players are more memorable to the pit boss, so they "need" TMS.21 to make sure everyone is getting the comps that he deserves. Yeah, right! TMS.21 is capable of so much more than just ascertaining comp value. At its heart, it is a devastatingly effective method of guaranteeing the maximum possible house advantage by calculating when high-count decks become cost prohibitive, as well as identifying skilled players before they can cause any potential damage to the casino coffers. That's an awfully powerful comp tally machine! Though facing many court challenges, it is still in use and growing in popularity with the casinos every day.

## CONTINUOUS-SHUFFLE MACHINES

A much more common — but just as devious — anti-counter device is called a Continuous-Shuffle Machine, or CSM. You'll notice these gizmos mounted on blackjack tables in place of the more traditional multi-deck shoes. Between hands, the dealer will collect that round's cards and dump them unceremoniously into the back of the machine, instead of into the traditional discard tray: Voilà, a brand-new, freshly shuffled shoe! Since card counting at its soul gains greater accuracy as more cards are seen before a dealer shuffle, CSMs actively defeat an advantage player's ability to gain any kind of an edge through counting. Normally, a dealer reshuffles every few hands (for a single-deck game) or after a certain number of decks have been dealt (in the case of a shoe game); CSMs create a completely new shuffle after *every* hand, minus any time and effort from the dealer. The cover story (ah, there's always a cover story, isn't there?) used to explain these electronic edge-killers is that they make game play faster (and therefore "better") for casino patrons due to the time saved by not manually shuffling multiple decks of cards. The reality is that precisely *because* players see about 20% more hands per hour at a CSM table — and because no realistic system for getting an advantage at that game exists — people end up *losing* much more money, much more quickly than at non-CSM tables. Thanks for the awesome hook-up, Mr. Casino! You rock!

This extra drain on the gaming public's bankrolls is accomplished in two devious ways: First, by dealing so many more hands per hour, the house's edge is magnified because of the direct correlation between house edge and player money lost per hour. For instance, a game with a 1% house edge where a player averages a $25 bet for 80 hands an hour (standard for hand-shuffled games) means an average player loss of $20 an hour (1% of $25 is 25 cents, times 80 hands, equals 20 bucks) — whereas at a CSM table, playing 96 hands an hour, that means an *additional* $4 loss per hour. What a great deal, huh?

The second way CSMs leech money from players is by severely limiting their comp dollars. As I mentioned in the section on TMS.21, the amount of complimentaries a player is entitled to is determined by correlating the average bet, length of play, and the house edge of the game being played. I'll get into comps more in the next chapter, but for now all you need to know is that a percentage of this final result is the player's total comp value, which can be used on food, rooms, show tickets, freebies, you name it … except, of course, when playing at a table with a CSM. CSMs actually *rob* people of the comps they have fairly earned as a result of their play because most casinos don't adjust their comp formula for CSM tables. This means that, even though patrons at those tables end up playing — and *losing* — more than at other tables, they are not credited for this additional action. What seems at first to be only a minor consideration actually turns into quite a tidy sum! One would think the house would just automatically make the simple adjustments needed to accurately determine true comp value at CSM blackjack tables, but alas, they're just another footnote in the long list of casino greed run amuck.

## GRIFFIN

As if everything discussed thus far weren't enough for you, I've yet to dissect the most diabolical, ruthless, and practically criminal anti-card-counter plot of all: Griffin. That one word is sure to strike terrifying fear into the hearts of advantage players everywhere. The Griffin Detective Agency began harmlessly enough in Las Vegas in the mid-1960s as a small detective service imbued with the noble mission of tracking cheaters, card mechanics, and other gambling scam artists for its prize clients, the casinos. A subscription-based service cataloging the aforementioned undesirables was made available and quickly became a staple of casino surveillance departments everywhere; that way, a guy who was caught cheating in Atlantic City, for instance, couldn't just cruise into a little riverboat gambling den on the Mississippi without being spotted there as well. As Griffin grew larger and figured more prominently into casinos' game protection strategies, it was only natural for the agency to branch out and provide another, more valuable, service — namely, the country's first comprehensive listing of card counters. As instrumental as Griffin had become in cataloging casino cheats, the compiling of counters (and other legal advantage players) was to eventually form the crowning triumph of Griffin's burgeoning empire. It was only a matter of time before massive demand for this feature solidified the agency's reputation as the primary, indispensable source of information in the war against professional gamblers.

Initially a short list containing only the most notorious advantage players, the casinos' insatiable obsession with eliminating all possible threats to the bottom line has ushered in Griffin's current era of xenophobic persecution. This discriminatory practice of creating longer and more detailed lists of players, whose only crime lies in using their brains, has turned full-throttle into an unchecked, rampant witch-hunt. While one could argue that casinos have every right to access this kind of database, what is inherently faulty about the Griffin system is that, in an effort to respond to such a frenzied demand for continually new and updated information, raw quality is sacrificed for a constantly renewable, mass quantity of names. Players barely dabbling as counters, people on vacation who manage to win a sizable chunk of money while betting unusually, and amateur counters who, left unchecked, would manage to lose far more than they could possibly gain, now find themselves all suspect.

Like the McCarthy communism hearings of the 1950s, the Griffin Agency is an equal opportunity criminalizer; it goes without saying that, once you're in the Griffin book, your days of playing are made *much* more difficult. The really horrible aspect of this discrimination is that it truly violates the civil rights of those listed; there is no court to appeal to, no pleading of your case, no "credit score" to build back up — once you've been "Griffinized," you're done. Some players manage to spend a lifetime in disguise or make short, sporadic hit-and-run attacks on tiny off-Strip casinos — or better yet, travel abroad to gambling halls that are far off the grid. What began in earnest as a couple of concerned detectives helping casinos identify *true* cheats has evolved into one of the most nefarious machinations of the gambling climate today, firmly entrenched in the vast network of casino surveillance operations.

In this modern age of computer control, the final *coup de grâce* is the creation of GOLD (Griffin On-Line Database), a completely automated online service dedicated 24/7 to assisting the casinos in their mission to eradicate the last vestiges of card counters from the earth. Not only does GOLD provide unlimited and immediate digital access to photos, bios, and background information on all its "suspects," it can identify a person as a subject of interest without even knowing the person's name. It works by letting surveillance personnel instantly search the database by entering a few search words, like "male, blonde, 26, blackjack, 5 feet 8 inches," and a list of suspects culled from thousands of photos and descriptions of slot cheats, card counters, and assorted grifters fills the screen.

## EVEN MORE COUNTERMEASURES

Once a casino has decided, through whatever means, that you're quite obviously a total dick intent on using your brain to take their money, you'll quickly find yourself the lucky recipient of generous amounts of casino attention. Namely, one of several tried-and-true countermeasures designed specifically to halt your mounting attack on their oh-so-fragile house of cards. With casinos, even the process of getting heat from the various pit critters (whose *job* it is to fuck with you) has been turned into a game. Rather than just walk up to you and say, "Hey, you suck, please leave" (although it certainly can escalate to that point), the floormen in your area will usually have fun playing all sorts of cruel tricks on you first.

One surefire crowdpleaser is the previously mentioned preferential shuffle. With this tactic, the pit boss will wait until you've jumped up to a bigger bet, then tell the dealer to shuffle the cards early and see how you react. Pulling your bet back looks suspicious, but leaving several betting units on the line for freshly shuffled cards is just bad EV. Have fun with this quandary!

Other savvy gimmicks they'll pull include dealing around you (i.e., dealing cards to all the players at the table except you, often with no explanation given), suddenly notifying you that from now on you can't bet over a certain miniscule amount (a popular move in Atlantic City, this is called being "flat-bet"), and every card counter's favorite: suddenly moving the cut card so far forward in the shoe that the penetration level goes out the window. These are just a few of the fun "games" that casinos use to tell you in no uncertain terms to fuck off, without actually saying, "Hey you — fuck off," much as they may want to. Nice, huh?

For those of you steadfast (read: stupid) enough to ignore these rising levels of heat, playtime is soon over and the real sanctions ensue. Getting backed off can certainly be worn as a badge of honor the first time or two it happens, since it confirms that you are a card counter worthy of being a threat to the casinos, but you'll quickly learn how much this totally blows for your longevity in blackjack. Casinos are notorious for sending flyers around town to other operations, warning them of the predator in their midst. Plus, you'll find yourself added to just about every electronic database they can get their hands on, complete with full color pictures and a flattering bio. I'll go into much more detail in the next chapter about different types of backoffs and how you should conduct yourself through them, but for now all you need to know is that getting bounced from a property is totally lame and more likely to occur the more time you give the casino to watch your gameplay. Pretty shitty cost of doing business, I know.

## THE FINAL FRONTIER

Casinos have increasingly pushed the limits of what they can get away with until there are virtually no playable games left, either through extreme rules variations or by simply upgrading surveillance to be so sensitive to potential card counters that the very act of winning money actually makes one a suspect. What's even crazier is that I've been thrown out of casinos many times when actually *down* money — as much as $20,000! Casinos sell the illusion that anybody can win; the reality is that even *potential* winners are immediately marked as possible cheaters. But the ultimate problem is simply in the general public's being *uninformed*. That is how the casinos keep their power and continually pull the wool further over the eyes of gamblers, year after year. The only real solution is to arm yourself with knowledge about what games to play (and which to *avoid* like the plague — 6:5 payouts, TMS.21 tables, and CSMs), combine that with a working knowledge of effective advantage plays, and above all, be *proactive* and educate everyone you possibly can about the horrible corporate swindle being foisted upon us all.

It is only through mass public awareness — by personally taking it upon ourselves to tell everybody we possibly can to stay away from these unfair games — that we will ever hope to stem the tide of casino greed run amuck and reclaim a fair gaming environment. While you're at it, be sure to check out my friend Norm Wattenberger's website at http://www.blackjack-scams.com/ (the name kind of says it all). There you'll learn of a whole slew of unplayable games and other casino countermeasures, including the ones I've mentioned here. I can teach you how to count cards, but that's a temporary solution at best; the following pages are filled with a wealth of information on avoiding the casino's ever-increasing "game protection" fanaticism, but the underlying problem of rampant corporate greed will only get worse. The only real, permanent solution lies in somehow bringing back the great boycott of Thorp's day and giving these corrupt casinos and unfair games the best advantage play of all: deserted tables.

And so it is into this seemingly hopeless police state that I now deliver you. But don't throw in the towel yet! Because when things seem most hopeless, when it feels the game itself has been completely thwarted by nearly insurmountable obstacles, when the chips are down and the stakes are high — it is *here* that your true training kicks in. You have met the enemy, and it is, shall we say, "unfriendly." It will stop at nothing to prevent you from succeeding, at all costs. It's awful, I know. But you're strong. You're different. You can do this. You must take everything they throw your way and adapt to it. Change. Grow. Defeat. Conquer. It CAN be done. Read on to discover how.

# Keeping It on the Down Low 6.

**Oh. My. God.** This is a HUGE chapter, people. But it's not about the size — it's how you use it that matters! Whole books are devoted to the camouflage aspect of advantage play because, without this skill, none of the painstaking effort you've put into becoming a genuine, card-counting math nerd matters. Here's the truth, in a nice, easy-to-swallow pill: It doesn't mean shit if you can count down a deck in 11 seconds flat, make true count conversions in the blink of an eye, and memorize 500 indices overnight *if you can't get away with it.* That's right — everything you've just spent months training for and perfecting is absolute garbage if you don't learn how to hide what you know from the casinos. Pretty lame, I know, but it's the reality we live in.

Remember, blackjack is dead — or certainly well on its way — due to the siege inflicted on it daily by overzealous casino operators and their henchmen. The essential fallacy inherent in the struggle of the modern-day advantage player is that they are despised, hunted, and killed by the same giant gaming machine that feeds them — blackjack giveth and blackjack taketh away. At least figuratively, in the sense that many of their playing careers are ended prematurely due to the incredible amounts of persecution that target those who do *not* effectively camouflage their mental skills. This damned paradox will face you every time you set foot in a gambling hall, and it must become a lifelong lesson in obsession for those of you who survive the initiation period and truly become the new breed of professional blackjack players.

The first step in concealing what you have worked so hard to learn is to simply understand what it is that looks so suspicious about what we do, and — just as importantly — how the casinos will react when they spot you doing it. And believe me, they *will* spot you, sooner or later. It is foolish to think that simply because they can't actually hear your inner thoughts — you know, the ones that keep the running count, do TC conversions, and plot to take over the world on a regular basis — they can't figure out exactly what you're doing, given enough time. The sad truth is that the vast majority of ploppies playing blackjack have no fucking clue what they're doing; their lack of basic strategy knowledge immediately clears them of any suspicion. Sure, most people have a general idea of BS — doubling down on elevens or splitting aces, for example — but when it comes to the more obscure plays like splitting nines or doubling on soft totals, players who consistently demonstrate knowledge of the correct play mark themselves as potential threats to the house. Play well, and they *will* notice.

Someone who has all the aspects of BS memorized sticks out like a sore thumb in the casino environment, and so the real trick of camouflage lies in the ability to completely emulate the appearance of the typical devil-may-care voodoo gambler while still retaining all the knowledge and edge of a true advantage player. Harder to do than it sounds; your actions always speak louder than your words, attitude, or win/loss rate. I've been thrown out of casinos while *losing* money; once they suspect you of being a counter, nothing else matters. You must learn to play this eternal game of cat and mouse — trying to make as much money as possible without getting thrown out in the process!

Barring suspected counters is what casinos do best, so to have the longevity you need in order to show a profit playing blackjack, you must learn a series of tactics that conceal your skills. Perhaps the toughest — and most paradoxical — element of good camouflage is that we must resist the temptation to haphazardly misplay our hands, because even though that is the best way to blend in with our surroundings, once we do it we are no longer playing with an edge. That means we're losing money, like everyone else. Which defeats the whole point of being an advantage player in the first place, doesn't it? Although there are certain rare situations that I'll discuss later in which an intentional misplay buys us more cover than the actual loss to our bottom line, good camouflage lies in applying specific techniques in order to get away with what we know without giving up too much EV in the process. Get the casinos off our backs, so we can get the maximum bang for our gambling buck. You ready? Let's do this.

## I'm not a dealer, I just play one on TV

Early in my blackjack career I worked a few private parties as a dealer, although I've never had any formal training or employment at an actual casino. One such party was a corporate affair at which Donna Summer was the surprise guest. Aside from how awesome it was to see her perform in such a tiny venue, I also learned something pretty valuable that night, which has stuck with me ever since. A few hundred casual players sat at my table over the course of the night and, as is typical of most blackjack enthusiasts, none of them had any clue whatsoever how to play the game. Ignorant, every single one of them. Or should I say, all except one: A single guy stood out from the hundreds, and do you know why? He was the *only* one in that entire crowd who actually knew basic strategy. It took my dealing just a few hands to him to notice it, and a few hands later my suspicions were confirmed. I followed along with the count to see if he was also making the appropriate betting decisions and playing deviations, but he wasn't. And, even though he wasn't a counter, it was immediately obvious to me that this guy was different. Imagine this same scenario on your next casino visit, in which you play the part of the lone guy in the crowd who plays perfect BS. Feel the heat radar rising already? You should. Terrifying, isn't it?

## THE EMPEROR'S NEW CLOTHES

One word: vigilance. That's camouflage lesson number one, and to embrace it fully you must forever adjust your perception of what it means to be a casino patron. Your innocence is officially over — from now on, every single time you enter a gaming establishment, you are the enemy. You heard me. If you think for one minute that those thousands and thousands of cameras, surveillance workers, pit bosses, computer tracking programs, and security personnel are only there to keep the games safe from cheaters and thieves, you are sadly mistaken! The single biggest reason all of those prevention methods exist is to stop you from achieving the nefarious goal of winning money. Bizarre, I know, considering the casinos' multi-million dollar ad campaigns to the contrary, but trust me when I say you've got a major battle on your hands now. If the casinos could put an IQ restriction on their patrons, they most certainly would; nobody over 90 gets in the door without first reporting to electroshock therapy. Bastards.

But I digress. Vigilance is to be your mantra from this point forth — a constant, ever-present awareness of your surroundings in casinos, and a general mindset from which stems the rest of camouflage theory. The most important aspect of camouflage is to develop a radar-like awareness for "heat." Heat is defined as the measure of casino awareness to your presence as an advantage player in their midst. It is your job to watch for it; keep it as low as possible; and disappear before it gets too high, the hammer comes down, and you find yourself out on the sidewalk, no longer welcome back. Like fossil fuels, casinos are a non-renewable energy source — every joint you burn through and find yourself barred from is one fewer blackjack game you have available to play in a world of rapidly diminishing playable games.

Advantage play is a never-ending battle between heat and longevity: Burn through enough casinos and you will no longer have the means to apply your craft to extract any more money from the house. As a new counter, you have the luxury of being unknown to the vast surveillance network that makes up casino game protection: Do your best to keep it that way. Anonymity protects us and keeps us safe; wrap yourself in the cloak of obscurity and present to them the image of what they most want to see: another slow, stupid, fun-lovin', easy-spendin' tourist out for a night on the town.

## Anonymity

I've lost my anonymity: If I didn't give it up when I landed on TV taking my shot at the *World Series of Blackjack* title over the past few years, I certainly traded it in to harass the stars on *Celebrity Blackjack,* rant at poker pros on *King of Vegas,* and run my mouth on the *Ultimate Blackjack Tour.* That's why I think the world's best blackjack player is still unknown! Why come out of hiding and into the limelight for a shot at a quick buck when it will effectively destroy the one thing APs prize above all else: anonymity. So why have many established authors and other public gambling figures that have lived the life in the trenches crossed over to public play? Many were banned from too many casinos or just got tired of hiding in the shadows all the damn time, but there are other reasons as well. For me, being an actor comes first and foremost, no matter how good I've become at cards. It's a personal choice, because I've always had the heart and soul of an artist, and originally started playing only as a survival gig.

So what does heat look like, exactly? Well, it really depends on what you're doing at the time. Heat can vary from something as simple as a pit boss casually watching your play to a cadre of security guards suddenly stationed at your table glaring at you, and everything in between. To be fair, since it is the casinos' job to protect their games, most gamblers receive *some* level of heat during the typical playing session. Don't start jumping at every sidelong glance a pit boss gives you just because you win a few hands in a row; notice instead the shift supervisor who answers a ringing phone in the pit suddenly turning to look directly at you, or a conference of several pit bosses near your table accompanied by furtive glances in your direction. Often these encounters are not cause for complete alarm or to get up and leave the premises, especially if the playing conditions are still right; however, with vigilance you will start to notice the escalating nature of the heat you receive and will develop a sense of when it is time to bail out on even the best of situations.

One thing that will help you determine how serious is the heat you're receiving (versus the mostly harmless kind you will encounter on a more frequent basis) is to observe how they react to specific situations. Certain plays draw much more attention to you than others do — namely, splitting tens when the count is high enough, doubling down on high soft totals (like soft 19 or 20), and taking insurance on crappy hands with big bets out. These are plays that average players almost never make, so if you have already established yourself as someone who knows BS cold and then you pull out one of these little beauties (which is bound to happen over the normal course of play), keep an eye out for any of the natives who may start to get a little too restless!

Another big heat magnet is wild bet spreads — such as when the count suddenly jumps skyward and your next bet is five times higher than the previous one. This looks suspicious because the typical gambler generally follows predictable betting patterns, raising and lowering bets to mirror the win/loss results of the last few hands. That is, after winning or losing the previous hand or series of hands, a gambler usually makes a predictable adjustment to the next bet. As counters, we recognize that whether we just won or lost has no bearing on the next result, so you can imagine how strange it looks when somebody betting the $25 table minimum ten hands in a row suddenly jumps his bet to two hands of $150!

Another way to be vigilant is to recognize how gamblers typically act, and then be observant of how the pit reacts to your not following that established pattern. To see what I mean, try this fun exercise out for shits and giggles: Hang out at a casino bar (preferably on a day when you're not playing, so you can get loaded on Singapore Slings with Mescal on the side) and watch the interaction between average gamblers and pit bosses. See how they relate to one another; remembering these behavioral norms helps keep you alert to when the scenario at your next table goes too far off-course.

## COVER PLAYS

Some casinos are more tolerant than others when it comes to heat, but there are many cover plays you can use to mitigate the more blatant moves you will be making as an advantage player. A good counter should have an arsenal of these little countermeasures stocked away for easy use while plundering blackjack riches.

### Rat-Holing Chips

Rat-holing is a funny name for a particularly devious play. This refers to the act of sneaking a few of your higher-denomination chips off the table as you start raking in the dough in order to give the appearance of not having won quite so much. Sounds childish, I know, but it helps cut down on a considerable amount of heat. That way, when you make some crazy plays or win a series of big bets when the count is high, you don't look like you're taking the casino for so much of a ride. Pit bosses will sweat your action periodically throughout your session, and more so when you are winning or making crazy plays that they do not attribute to your being a complete donkey; not having as much money in front of you to show for it goes a long way in allaying the pit critters' concerns.

The best way to rat-hole chips is to slip one or two into your palm while you're adjusting your chip stacks between bets, then make an inconspicuous move to your pocket or purse to pull out a cell phone, watch, tissue, or some other such justifiable item. If you just jam your hand in your pocket when the dealer isn't looking without any discernible reason for doing so, you're forgetting about the zillions of cameras and other casino personnel that are quite capable of more clandestinely observing your every move.

Depending on the type of table you're at and how many chips of what denomination you have in front of you, you want to sneak off just enough of the bigger chips so as not to diminish the physical size of your stack, while making sure their absence will have a significant effect on the total monetary value left in front of you. If you're at a $5 table with $200–$300 of nickels and quarters in front of you (slang for $5 and $25 chips), rat-hole a few quarters. At a $25 table with $700–$800 in front of you, make a couple of black chips ($100s) disappear. This cover play is especially valuable when you are leaving a table and the dealer goes to color you up (trading in your lower denomination chip stack for just a few higher denomination chips); the dealer will usually announce the total to the nearest floorman, which clearly shows them that you didn't make nearly as much money as they thought you did.

## "Rain Man"

I never know what characters I'll run into during the many home poker games I play in Hollywood. One such game was $1/$2 Stud, with the likes of Mimi Rogers, Ed Asner, Lou Gossett, Jr, Camryn Manheim, Chris Noth, James Woods, and Julianna Margulies. What caught my attention (even more than the fact these millionaires play for such low stakes, with no checkraising allowed — hey, it's a friendly game) was a story Mimi Rogers told me about her blackjack experience. Apparently, she learned how to count cards while then-hubby Tom Cruise was filming his role in *Rain Man,* and spent every day at Caesars Palace playing with impunity. Talk about amazing cover — who's going to throw out a famous movie star for counting cards? What a PR nightmare that would be! Mimi swore she never lost a session, and while I'm sure that wasn't always the case, she must've really cleaned out the place for the few weeks she was there. The lesson? Become a household name and you never have to worry about camouflage again!

There's also a flip side to this coin. If you hit a crappy sequence of cards and your buy-in gets wiped out, you can play up the part of the big loser while secretly chuckling about the money you've got stashed away, leaving the false impression of having "lost everything" back to the house. In either case, just make sure that you cash out at the cage only for the amount the pit thinks you have, and come back on another shift to cash the rat-holed chips (or have a friend cash them); the pit and cage are in communication a lot more frequently than you might think, and if there's any discrepancy, the cashier's window is actually one of the best places for the casino to snap a clear, well-lit, high-res photo of you for what can only be described as illicit purposes! Carry the illusion away from the table with you; remember, there's always someone watching.

### Chip Comportment

Speaking of chips, we should address some other cover plays that have to do with their handling and use throughout your sessions. The key here is to not give the appearance of someone who has spent a lot of time around chips; that means no fancy shuffling tricks or nifty chip bounce moves like the poker pros use. Also, card counters tend to stack their chips in neat organized columns, whereas ploppies often sit in front of an unkempt pile of broken hopes and dreams, waiting for the voodoo luck of the card gods to send them a sign and spur them into action, shoving their chips out in haphazard fistfuls of drowning karma. Do as they do — keep messy, multi-denominational clusters of chips in front of you; not only does this make it easier to get away with rat-holing, but it sends the message that you are just there to gamble like a good little tourist. And the house will love you for it.

### Buying In

Money plays! Buying in to the game when you sit down is an important process and one that does not go unnoticed. The rule of thumb is to buy in for an amount typical to the limits of the table you are at, as well as what you look like you should be buying in for. For instance, don't sit down at a $10 table wearing casual clothes and smack $1,000 on the felt. This, needless to say, will give you immediate heat! At lower-limit tables (up to quarters), buying in for no more than 20 to 30 times the table minimum is plenty. In fact, since you are trying to emulate typical casino patrons, notice how many people either buy in for a single hundred-dollar bill, or some bizarre lower amount — like $40 at a $5 table. The one exception to this rule is if you are dressed very expensively (especially the watch and the shoes), or appear to be much older or more conservative; then you could get away with buying in for more without attracting too much heat. Even then, it's unnecessary. Once you are sitting at the $100 and above tables (with the appropriate bankroll to back it up, of course), feel free to buy in for much more — because giving the impression that you're a big whale about to lose your whole wad is exactly the kind of attention you do want!

### Disguising Bet Ramps

Nothing looks so artificial or screams for attention more than a guy who flat bets quarters for an hour and then suddenly spreads to two hands of $200! That, and someone who loses four hands in a row, then inexplicably triples his bet ... "Hi, I'll take 'instant heat' for $1,000 please, Alex." We must remember the voodoo manner in which most people bet: predictable patterns of bigger or smaller bets based on the results of previous hands, or some kind of stop-win/ loss (betting big until hitting a certain monetary profit or loss, then pulling back, for instance). So, without giving up your edge or deviating from the appropriate bet based on the current count, you must find a way to disguise your real betting logic. Here are a couple ideas, and I'm sure you can figure out a few on your own as well.

First up is a technique called "steaming," in which you emulate "the big loser" to justify why you are increasing your bet due to a skyrocketing count, in spite of a string of recent losses. The best way to get more money on the felt without arousing too much suspicion is to act as if you are quite literally steaming mad about losing so much, even going so far as to comment something like, "This time I'm gonna get you, dealer — you can't keep taking my money forever! All I need is to win this one and I'm even with you," as you shove a fistful of chips into the betting circle. To be successful, you mustn't act like you are joking — really get "upset" at the losses. Sell it, baby. "You jerks have had enough. Now it's my turn!" It goes without saying that you shouldn't try to pull this act off if you've won the hands before your big bet.

Another snazzy angle you can use to disguise your betting ramp is to employ the clever use of "rainbows." A rainbow is a bet consisting of a clump of multi-colored chips that still add up to a specific betting unit. For instance, let's say the count justifies a bet of three units on a particular hand (with $25 units, a bet of $75). Instead of putting three quarters on the felt, instead try using two quarters, four nickels, and five silver dollars; the total is still $75, but now you've convinced the pit critters that you're using some sort of strange superstitious betting system too bizarre for anyone but you to understand.

## Dealer Errors

Yes, dealer errors do happen, and more frequently than you might imagine. Despite the zillions of cameras and prying eyes, there are times when a hand motion is misunderstood, a winning bet is overpaid, or a losing hand is pushed instead of taken. Here's the age-old dilemma: Do you A) retain your inherent integrity, and let the house know when it is owed more money? Or B) feign ignorance and rake in your ill-gotten gains before anybody notices? This isn't a philosophical question people — there's only one right answer. Any guesses? Yes, you — you in the back there, reading in the easy chair while Flock of Seagulls rocks in the background — do you know the answer? Ding, Ding, Ding ... Yes, you're absolutely right! If the rest of you also answered "B) Take the House's Fucking Money," then you're correct! Give yourself a pat on the back, and laugh at the sorry bastards who wanted to give the rotten casinos another hearty serving of their bankrolls. Seriously, what part of "the casinos don't play fair" don't you get? It's not a question of your ethics here, it's simply an expression of EV in a corrupt environment that tries every day and in every way to strip you of your money, intelligence, and dignity — and then dares to call it "protecting the integrity" of their games from the scourge of APs in their midst. Simply consider every extra payout and accidental push as payment for all the barrings, heat, camouflage, and discrimination you'll face in the pursuit of doing nothing more than using your brain while playing cards. Sorry, did that come across as a little harsh? Hey, what can I say? Sometimes the truth hurts.

Anytime you can add to the mystique of being a voodoo gambler, do it. Make the bastards chase you down the rabbit hole! Rainbows can also be used when the TC is stuck somewhere between two different unit bets; split the difference with random rainbow bets that add up to nonsensical numbers somewhere in the range of the appropriate unit bets (for instance, if the TC justifies a bet between two and three $25 units, shove something like $67 of odd chips into the betting circle). This feeds into your "loose gambler" image while actually giving you more accurate control over your bet ramp.

You can also tweak the power of rainbows by adding "caps" to your bets. Caps are last-minute additions to your bet, just under the wire of the close of betting for the current hand. One day at the MGM in Vegas, I had a dealer convinced I was some kind of holy roller because I would randomly select certain bets to cap with a silver dollar ("To ward off evil spirits. You understand, right?"), even going so far as to shout "Wait! This is the hand you pull a blackjack! Hold on, I gotta protect my cards!" and then throw a silver dollar down on top of my bet, just as she was about to start dealing. You'll probably end up pissing off a fair number of dealers with this tactic — they'll even go so far as to prevent you from capping certain bets in which you intentionally wait too long to make your move, especially if you try to cap by throwing out a quarter chip or higher — but one thing they'll probably never suspect you of is actually being intelligent enough to count cards!

### Intentional Misplays

Think of this as the advertising budget for your illicit AP business: You can't spend too much on it or you'll swallow up your narrow profit margin, but a few well-placed "ads" will only increase your long-term revenue. Intentionally misplaying key marginal hands, especially early in your session when pit critters and surveillance staff are diligently trying to classify your skill level, can go a long way in reducing your heat over the long run. Here are some marginal hands to look for: 16 against a dealer 10 — occasionally stand instead of hit or surrender; soft 15s, 16s, and 17s against dealer 3s and 4s — sometimes double down, sometimes hit; stand on a 12 against dealer

2s and 3s once in a while; and the most effective misplay — do something completely crazy (like hit a hard 13 against dealer 4s and 5s, or insure a good hand even when the count is low) when you have a minimum bet out. But remember, every time you make one of these plays, you are blatantly lowering your EV and effectively giving away your money; however, three or four of these types of plays early in a session (with smaller bets out) don't cost much but lay down excellent cover. Just make sure that it's ultimately worth it — wait until that pit boss is right there with you at the table, watching your play, and don't forget to sell it.

Gamblers are generally a friendly, superstitious bunch, so don't hesitate to ask for "advice" from the floorman or announce something like, "Last time I hit a 16 against a 10, I busted — so this time, I stand! Let's see how you like that, dealer!" You get the point. What sells these cover plays is the inconsistency with which they happen — unlike Illustrious 18 deviations due to the count, these types of plays do not seem to follow the standard AP modus operandi, and so give you the voodoo mystique of being just another crappy gambler, out for a night on the town. Casinos are an anomaly; they're the one place on earth where appearing "crappy" is actually a good thing!

### Dealer Shuffle Tricks

One of the biggest sore thumbs we as counters have is that we must see a certain number of cards in the deck or shoe before we have an idea of how much to bet. How do you think it looks to the house when, deep in a high count, you place a big bet and then, realizing the dealer needs to shuffle the cards, you pull the large wager back and replace it with a minimum bet? Awful, that's how! You might as well turn on a blinking neon sign over your head that says, "Card Counter" in bright, red letters. The obvious solution here is to just be aware of where the shuffle point is so that you won't be caught with your pants down, but a bigger lesson we can take from this is to not always start off freshly shuffled cards with a minimum bet out.

Despite the small disadvantage, sometimes you'll want to buy some cover by using a two- or two-and-a-half-unit bet off the top to break your pattern, even going so far as to occasionally leave the accidental big bet out you placed prior to the shuffle for the start of the new first hand. Rainbows come in handy here; you can take advantage of the shuffling pause to "rethink" a better voodoo bet and replace your accidental big bet with some strange concoction of smaller multi-colored chips that mimic your single-unit bet but don't appear to be motivated by the resetting of the count.

## Shitty Counts

A good way to offset the debilitating effects of playing through negative counts is to sit at a table with a minimum bet that is lower than your unit bet; for instance, playing a $10 game while using $25 units. That way you can bet less than a single unit when the TC goes too far south. Just make sure your bankroll size (and requisite RoR) is still set for the unit bet you're actually using, rather than the table minimum. Cool? Cool.

### Bathroom Breaks

Who would have thought that something your mother taught you as a child could save you so much money one day? Perfect for when the count plummets like a freight elevator with cut brakes descending straight into hell, this camo trick has saved more than one bankroll from certain destruction. The verity of counting is that the average count is zero; that means much of the time we are stuck in the rotten miasma of negative counts. Bet ramps take into consideration increasing betting units that correspond with higher and higher counts, but there are no safeguards for betting into very low numbers, since we are usually unable to bet fractions of our unit bet due to table minimums.

This is why you must get particularly creative when the count is down in the dumps; sometimes you can get away with sitting out until the next shuffle, but do that more than once or twice and you'll find your heat-meter rising. What makes finding camouflage methods for avoiding bad counts so imperative is the unfortunate tendency for shoes (much more so than single- or double-deck games) to go exceptionally positive or negative, and then stay that way. Once the true count gets to –3 or –4, I'm looking for a way out, especially if there are still a few decks to go. Remember, every hand you play during a negative count is a hand in which the house has the advantage. Advantage player urban legend has it that card counters possess the worst bladders in the world, and now you understand why!

Other popular methods of avoiding lower counts are: suddenly needing to take a cell phone call (away from the table, of course), steaming after a few bad hands and going to "walk it off," and — my personal favorite — going over to flirt with a particularly cute cocktail waitress or some other random casino hottie. Experimenting with different combinations of these suggestions (plus your own creative additions) will not only make a big difference to your bottom line, but will also keep the heat during your sessions down to much more manageable levels. Do whatever it takes to get The Man off your back.

### Fake Drinks, Anyone?

Repeat after me, you degenerate alcoholics: Do NOT drink when playing cards! I can't believe we made it this far without a rant from me on the subject, so let me say it again for the benefit of my fellow wine and bourbon enthusiasts: No drinksies while playing cardsies. Capiche? Believe me, nobody loves the taste of a sweet, sweet Manhattan on the rocks (with a dash of cherry juice straight from the garnish tray instead of the vermouth — try it, you'll like it) more than your narcissistic narrator, but never, never before — or during — a session. The simple fact is that, as card counters, we perform dozens of calculations and evaluations in our head every second and cannot afford to make any mistakes. Even though it may seem completely harmless to nurse a single beer over the course of a session to buy some camouflage (since the casinos know counters never drink), the truth is that even a single beer decreases your mental acuity and can lead to disastrous financial mistakes.

If you don't believe me, get yourself wrapped up in a tasty shoe game with a decent count, have a beer or two, and see what happens to your true count conversions. Notice how your perception of heat alters. And you'll realize that you just don't wanna fuck with the delicate and intricate balance of math, camouflage, and bankroll considerations that goes into a typical playing session. What's worse is when you don't even notice what aspects of the game you're missing until it's too late and the goons close in — or your bankroll disappears. Expensive drink there, buddy!

That being said, one of my favorite camo tricks is to bring a little hidden flask of apple cider with me to a casino, order a nice scotch or bourbon from the cocktail waitress after I buy into a table, then take a trip to the bathroom after it's been delivered and replace the liquor with the cider. Now you get to have fun acting like you're drunk at the table, which provides great cover for the crazier splits and double downs you must make at higher counts. Vegas loves a drunk ... the pit critters will mistake all your genius plays for sheer drunken stupidity; you simply can't buy that kind of cover!

### Acting, My Dear Boy

Another subject I know a thing or two about, and what can ultimately make living the deranged, underground life of a card counter pretty entertaining at times is to put the "fun" back in "dysfunctional." Acting embraces a whole gamut of camouflage techniques, and must cater to each individual's particular style and taste. This cover play involves crafting the very identity of the persona you present to the casinos the entire time you're on the gaming premises. Think of it as the justification for your very existence: Will you play the role of the "drunk" tourist, out for a wild night on the town? A wealthy businessman, leisurely spending a few hours away from his family? Or perhaps some hotshot trust-fund kid, too stupid to know the "right" way to play? The choice is yours, but just remember to *commit* to your decision or the reality of what you are really doing will catch up with you. The fact of the matter is that casinos are always looking to categorize their patrons — Tourist, Businessman, Punk Kid, etc. — so it is your job as an advantage player to give them what they need to see, so they rest easy and don't try to classify you into a more harmful category (Card Counter, Cheater, Bum ... You get the picture).

Get creative and find a role to act out, planning down to the last detail what you do for a living, where you live, what you're doing in town, stories you want to tell, and anything else that pertains to playing this part. Make sure you do your homework, in case someone at the table (or worse, a pit boss) used to live and work, etc. in the same place and wants to chat! Many times this character you invent can be who you really are outside of your advantage-player duties, but sometimes — due to profiling or past encounters at a casino — you may want to alter your identity to a certain extent.

A great AP and friend of mine who wrote *Blackjack Blueprint* and goes by the pseudonym Rick "Night Train" Blaine popularized a three-step litmus test for developing your background and cover story before entering a casino. First, your appearance *must match* the money you're spreading around — the more money you play with, the more expensive your clothes, shoes, watch, and accessories need to be, regardless of whether you're in a tailored business suit or a couture track suit. Secondly, know *where* you got the money you're spreading around — discretionary income? Dot-com millionaire? Inheritance? Come up with something, anything — just as long as it matches your appearance and cover story, and make sure to have all the details about your story down to a "T" in case a pit critter starts poking around about it. Finally, know *why* you're there, in that particular casino and city. Obviously, if you're in Vegas or Atlantic City, you can claim to be on vacation, but what happens when you're making moves overseas or Down Under? Vacation, sure, but not as likely as a business trip, visiting family (make sure you know the area if you use this one), and the like.

My favorite line, since I travel with money despite looking like a rock and roll punk, is that I'm scouting locations for a movie I'm producing. Either that, or I give them the vague but mysteriously intriguing, "I work in television." Could mean anything! Keep in mind, you want to make your story as simple as possible so you don't get tripped up; all you're looking to accomplish with this three-step litmus test is to justify yourself to the casino in those crucial first five seconds when you sit down at a table so that the house doesn't even begin to think you may be a thief, con man, or worse: a skilled professional player.

"Profiling" is an important consideration to take into account when deciding what character to become during your sessions; despite how politically correct corporations have become (officially, at least) in abolishing the discriminatory practices associated with gender and race, the fact remains that certain customer demographics receive much more heat from the house than others. An older Asian woman playing $100 a hand and spreading 1–10 barely catches a sidelong glance from the pit boss (save for a particularly rapacious look when she first pulls out her cash), but a white guy in his mid-20s who quietly sits down and pulls a hat over his eyes to play for the same stakes is immediately scrutinized within an inch of his life. I don't make the rules — in fact, I doubt many official documents exist outlining a concise system of company policy in this regard — but the reality is, these prejudices *do* exist and they are applied all the time.

## Blackjack Babes

Hot chicks are hardly ever suspected of doing the deed in a casino (card counting, silly — what were you thinking?), primarily because of the prejudice that exists about young hotties not being very smart. To the contrary, some of the world's best players are smoking hot chicks who profit with impunity off the casinos; in fact, a friend of mine who played with the MIT team for a time actually found that one of the more unusual forms of heat she received was not that she was suspected of being a card counter, but rather a hooker. Ouch! And the funny thing is that it was better the casinos think that than the real truth of the matter!

This is the casino's unofficial profile of a card counter: younger players are more suspect than older ones; men much more so than women; white people over any other race; quiet players before talkative ones; and overweight ahead of thin-and-trim. So if you're a thin Brazilian gentleman with a fascinating life story to share, play on — but if you happen to be a shy white college student who's a little overweight, you already have a couple of strikes against you! This is where the acting comes in really handy — you're not able to change your age, sex, or race very easily, but you can do a lot to counteract these casino prejudices by being aware of how your appearance influences the heat you receive and using this information to craft a persona that takes advantage of their preconceptions. Some pros who have built up a much larger bankroll or who have truly been living the AP lifestyle for years will develop entirely separate names and identities for use in the casinos, the legal ramifications of which are discussed in much more detail in other sources (again, check the reference section in back). This is one time when other people's prejudices can really work for you — turn the stereotyping around and use it against them!

### Disguises

Awww yeah, bitches — now we're talking serious camo! Generally for the more serious player (or those who've been caught and thrown out on more than one occasion), disguises are a valuable accessory in prolonging the longevity of your game, year in and year out. Wigs, fake glasses, facial hair, and the clever use of makeup can all be exploited to change your appearance and help you live a full nine lives in the casinos. As long as the final result doesn't look fake (unless that is your intention, as in gaudy costume jewelry or bad toupees over obviously bald crowns), the sky's the limit here, folks.

A few simple rules of thumb, for those who plan to use just a piece or two of disguise when playing: Except for silly party hats or a 10-gallon cowboy hat that completes a Western outfit, hats are generally a bad idea — especially baseball caps — because they make you look like someone who doesn't want to be recognized. Which is what card counters do, right? Right. Try to come up with items that support a believable story or character you're using — anything to throw attention away from advantage play and on to something else. A genius piece of disguise is a convention nametag. Try to scam one of these little beauties from a big conference or convention in town, and voilà — instant disguise: You're now John Dicknut from Tuscaloosa, in town for the power tool conference. Changing something simple like your facial hair or glasses can really go a long way in altering your appearance. Just be careful to pay attention to the details — your watch and shoes should always match the rest of your outfit. Nothing looks more out of place than a "businessman" in a suit wearing scuffed black loafers and a cheap watch, or a casually dressed youngun showing up with a Rolex strapped to his wrist (unless you have some killer story about being the disenchanted Prince of Arabia or some shit).

In terms of profiling, casinos have certain preconceived notions about what counters are "supposed" to look like as well — generally, someone who is casually attired gets much more attention than one who is dressed for a night on the town or some type of career function (convention, meeting, etc). Really, "disguise" is a misleading word because this camouflage technique involves your physical appearance no matter if it's a crazy clown suit or just your favorite pair of jeans and a t-shirt. The most important consideration when selecting what outfit, disguise, or accessories to wear is that your overall image must match the cover story and character you've chosen to portray. You wouldn't call yourself a doctor and then come dressed like a punk rocker, so if you've chosen to act the role of the wealthy socialite wife of a stock broker out for a night of fun playing hundred dollar chips while the husband sleeps, you better make damn well sure you're wearing Prada and are covered in real diamonds, girlfriend.

Strangely enough, the best disguises don't shun attention as much as *attract* it. Another friend of mine, a famous author and gambling personality, who is recognized in most casinos, is still a very active advantage player despite how difficult it would seem for him to play unnoticed. One of his best disguises involves dressing head-to-toe in full cowboy regalia, complete with a huge cowboy hat, leather vest, and riding chaps. To top it off, he grows a beard and acts like a crazy tourist, whooping and hollering every time he wins a hand, and talking non-stop about his ranch back home. You can't miss him — but would be shocked to know who he really is. This kind of "hiding out in the open" is sometimes the most effective, allowing you to hit and run without the house ever realizing it's just been taken!

## OTHER GOODIES

### Tokes

That's "dealer tips" to you cheapskates out there. Here's a joke from old advantage-player lore: "What's the difference between a card counter and a canoe? Sometimes a canoe tips!" Hilarious, I know, but there's definitely a grain of truth in there somewhere. As an AP, you must adopt a vigilant stance toward toking, and I'll tell you why. Despite the tendency by many players (and the urging of many toke-hustling dealers) to tip after winning a big hand or series of hands, remember that you are lucky to make 1%–2% on average from card counting. Not much, is it? So if you're betting quarters at 80 hands an hour, you're putting roughly $2,000 on the felt and have an EV of $20–$40. So what happens if you toke a couple of nickels during that hour? BAM — there goes your profit. Yes, it really is that serious — you simply can't afford to give away your EV or you will never make money in the long run! This is what prompts many APs to completely shun tipping under any circumstances, at any time. Naturally, you can understand their hesitation.

There are, however, a few instances in which toking should be encouraged. Primarily you must be aware that tokes can be used to "buy" better penetration from certain savvy dealers. It's not a particularly common occurrence, but it is something you should always be on the lookout for. It works like this: Make a couple of lighthearted references to the shoe (or decks) being "hot" and wanting to keep playing. Gauge the dealer's response. If the dealer seems receptive, a well-timed toke can keep a hot count going for an extra few hands. Obviously, in the case of many games these days, a cut card comes up to let the dealer know it is time to shuffle. Toking for penetration may lose the battle but win the war, as a dealer who is responsive to this type of negotiation may still reshuffle the current round early, but then place the cut card deeper after the shuffle so that the next round of play runs longer. If you're lucky enough to find this type of dealer, keep him/her well lubricated with a toke or two just before the shuffle point to ensure deeper penetration. Sometimes this technique works because the dealer knows more about counting than others and figures one hand washes the other, but unfortunately this behavior is lost on the majority of dealers, and you should immediately suspend any further toking should they prove to be unresponsive. Let them feel like they are on your winning "team" and make them work for their tips!

Another effective point at which to toke is when you're

trying to counteract a sudden rise in the heat level you're experiencing at the table. Maybe you just split tens and got a concerned look from the pit boss; maybe the count is so low that you're hitting 12s and 13s in ways you normally don't; or maybe you lost six hands in a row but the count just skyrocketed so now you've spread to two hands of eight-unit bets. In any of these cases, announcing that you're gonna take care of the dealer is a good way to "soften the blow" of your actions — especially since everybody "knows" card counters don't tip, so you must not be doing anything wrong. Again, if the toke has little or no effect, suspend it immediately and save the EV! You may also be thinking of cutting your session short and bailing before the heat gets too intense. When and if you do decide to leave (due to excessive heat or just because your session length has expired), you may also consider tossing out a "thank you" toke for the dealer out of sheer generosity (keep in mind, this does have a very real effect on your EV since most counters do not develop this kind of sympathy for the "enemy") or, more importantly, to preserve some kind of table image with a particular dealer for a future session. Bottom line on toking, you must do it only for specific reasons and at specific times, and cancel the action if it does not immediately procure the results you're after. It sounds callous, but thinking in this way will ensure that you keep the majority of your long-term profits, and shows you just don't fuck around as an advantage player.

Sometimes a well-timed toke can shut up a nosy dealer who is about to rat you out to his pit boss! Recently, I was in Vegas on a business trip (read: whoring myself out to the ladies) and met up with my manager (hey, it's an L.A. thing — we all have our own personal managers, agents, lawyers, publicists, and hairstylists) at the Imperial Palace cocktail lounge for the express purpose of downing sake and figuring out where the night would take us. He had started early, and drunkenly insisted that we play blackjack so that he could mimic my bets and make some money. I rarely get the luxury of playing anymore, because it's only a matter of time before I'm spotted (thanks to the Molotov cocktail combination of Griffin and television exposure) and thrown out. However, he kept insisting and eventually I relented because, after all, this was the Imperial Palace; I mean, who cares, right?

So I jumped my bets crazily as the count fluctuated, splitting and doubling down with no regard for laying down cover plays first, and even went so far as to advise my manager how to play his hands so as to give him the biggest edge possible. As the chips started to roll in, I noticed the dealer getting more and more uncomfortable with what was so blatantly happening in front of him; his pit boss was occupied elsewhere and the casino was stuffed full of rambunctious, weekend warriors out for some drunken craziness. Finally, he couldn't take it anymore, and after I split a pair of tens into a high count, he blurted out "You know you shouldn't be doing that, right?" He turned to alert the closest pit critter when I exclaimed, "You're right, it's awful. Share the wealth, that's what I say!" and dropped a nickel chip on the toke line for him. What did I care? I had already tripled my buy-in, the count was something like +10, I was betting 12 units, and I wanted to play out the rest of the double deck before the ride came to a complete and grinding halt.

Greed flickered in his eyes (hey, $5 goes a long way at the IP) and I knew I had him; he dealt me a pair of 8s, which I promptly split (adding another nickel toke to the second wager), and I received a 10 on one 8 and a 3 on the other. A double down (and another nickel toke) later, I was sitting pretty while the dealer busted and I cleaned up on the very profitable hand. As the dealer paid his tokes off, I winked and got up from the table. "Glad to have you on the payroll," I said mischievously, "Don't worry, I'll throw – I mean, show — myself out!"

## Session Length

So you're cruising along playing some mythical single-deck game with 90% pen, the pit bosses are all out to lunch, you're splitting tens and insuring stiffs with impunity, and the dealer keeps falling asleep at the wheel, paying you on almost every push. An hour goes by, then two, and suddenly the TC on the deck skyrockets to +20! You have virtually no heat and spread to three hands of 12-unit bets when abruptly — Tap, Tap, Tap. Out of nowhere, a shift supervisor and three goons appear behind you unannounced and throw you out of the joint, dispassionately ignoring your pleas of innocence. Suddenly, all your former glee is replaced by dread as you realize that not only have you been spotted, but now your snapshot is being placed in the Griffin book of card counters, cheats, and other casino undesirables. Way to go, Captain Obvious.

The lesson here is to set — and respect — session limits, no matter how lucrative the game. The first thing to consider when deciding how long to stay is to appraise how playable the game is. Realistically, you wouldn't even sit at a table in the first place if it didn't pass the initial screening criteria for pen depth, rules variations, crowd density, and the like. Beyond that, you have to use your best judgment to determine how much heat you're receiving and how the house is sweating your action. Eventually you'll develop a pretty accurate radar for this, and you'll just know when it's time to get the hell out. Assuming that your cover plays are keeping the heat level low, the other major consideration you need to heed is time. It is most certainly your enemy, and after a set period of time, you have to go, no matter how good the game.

Why? Well, what do you think happened to the protagonist in the little story I told you a minute ago, about the sudden tap on the shoulder in an otherwise heatless, perfect game? I'll tell you — camera surveillance. It's the most insidious and uncontrollable form of heat, and one that you will never even see coming, barring the occasional tip-off phone call to the pit. Don't ever forget that every second you spend in a casino is subject to the secret, prying eyes of the surveillance staff; once you sit down, it only gets worse. Your every bet and playing decision are offered up for cross-examination by a devilish mixture of analytical computer programs and cold-blooded specialists whose sole job is to determine if you're a skilled player intent on mischief or just a harmless idiot being primed for the kill. A smart counter is always aware of this harsh reality and knows that every moment spent on camera gives the hidden surveillance team a longer rope to hang you with.

Assuming you're keeping a lid on any excess heat, your session length should fall somewhere between 45 minutes and an hour. That's it, folks. The big factor influencing exactly when in that timeframe you actually take off depends, honestly, on how many advantage plays you pull in that period of time. If the count stays somewhere around the neutral point for the first half hour you're there, well, obviously you're not making any of the wild betting spreads or strange playing decisions that would give surveillance a reason to consider you anything but a basic strategy player. If, in the first five minutes of sitting down, however, the count skyrockets and you start raking in the dough, watch out. Too much attention means that even a 45-minute session may be stretching things a bit; again, use your best judgment. In fact, we should all be so lucky to have a relatively uneventful session for the first 15 minutes; by this point, the surveillance team has probably already classified you as a non-threat and you can most likely play past the hour mark. You'll get a better sense of your session length as time goes on, but erring on the side of caution more often than not will save you a lot of EV in the long run!

The big benefit of playing in crowded cities like Las Vegas is that you will have more casinos to play at — so you can go hit up another joint for some action after your session at one establishment expires. You should play no more than one session at any given casino per shift (so that you will be evaluated by different sets of eyes), and no more than once every day or two if you've received any kind of serious heat while playing (again, on a different shift as the previous session). Shifts work the same in casinos as they do anywhere else; day shift, swing shift, and graveyard shift. The exact shift change hours may vary from joint to joint, but hang out at a casino long enough and you'll notice when the pit bosses swap out. Often, the surveillance personnel will shift change an hour later than the pit critters, so be aware of that tricky little maneuver and plan your sessions accordingly. A really great online resource for planning out the different sessions you will play over a trip can be found at www.Trackjack.com. It's an online database of blackjack playing conditions all over the world, and is continually updated by a legion of loyal APs so as to present the most accurate information possible. That way, before you take off to Vegas for a week of advantage play you can check and see where the best pen can be found, which casinos are offering optimal rules variations, and other newsworthy headlines. It's one of the most valuable secret weapons in the underground fight against the machine, and something no AP should be without!

## Other APs

Don't be a jerk. If you run into other counters during a game, don't draw any attention to it. I get it — you're a member of an elite band of blackjack mercenaries and sometimes it gets lonely out there behind the iron curtain. You've got the skills to identify another counter in seven minutes flat, and want to share in the camaraderie with a fellow advantage player. Well, don't. APs are a particularly paranoid bunch and will only freak out and disappear at the very indication that you know what they're doing. And yes, this includes talking in cleverly coded phrases like "Uts-way e-thay ount-cay?" Seriously, dude: The fastest way to convince a fellow counter that you are actually a spy sent by casino surveillance intent on taking him out back and roughing him up is to try to make contact with him. And, to be quite honest, you should react the exact same way if someone else at a table tries to engage in "shop talk" with you, even after you've walked away from the game. The casinos spend wads of money every year on anti-counter personnel, programs, and other dissuasion methods. Therefore, your very first thought when some kindly old gentleman tells you he's been watching you play and that he's a counter, too, should be to Deny, Deny, Deny and get the hell out. Hone those instincts; they will save your blackjack career one day.

If you're really set on getting to know your fellow APs, there are much safer ways than while on the job. Many online gambling bulletin board sites have really flourished in the past decade, becoming a mainstay for information exchange and education as well as fostering a sense of community between geographically disparate and clandestinely challenged individual players. Where else can you participate in an online discussion or leave a private message for the most prolific authors and minds of our industry, and learn from the experiences of the world's best players?

There are several reputable sources (and a whole helluva lot of crap sites) out there, and I've included a reference of the best online communities in the resource section at the back of this book. Most of the good sites are headed up by a particular author or authority in the gambling world, and to that end you can rest assured that the standards associated with the content and characters on the site benefit from the reputation of its patron. Still, caution must be exercised in these semi-public forums, as many casino trolls regularly peruse the posts there to learn anything they can to aid in their quest to shut down the AP community. Take everything with a grain of salt, and recognize that relationships between professional gamblers take a very long time to develop; once you make a few good contacts, more will follow. I spent years as a card counter scraping together money for my rent and bills before I had any real contact with other APs — just a series of online posts and messages, but no solid friendships. The longer you pursue this unconventional career and stay in the energy of being an advantage player, the more relationships you will attract and the more rewarding the lifestyle will be. Only the strong survive ... but we band together for strength. Us against them, until the end.

### Wonging

Ah, wonging. Let's all bow our heads for a moment of silent prayer and contemplation as I invoke the name of the once and future king, Stanford Wong: herald of heralds, he whose name echoes in the hallowed corridors of blackjack lore. You've just gotta be The Man to get a move named after you. Maybe one day I'll get a cool blackjack move of my own, but until then, this one will have to do. "Wonging" is accomplished by waiting near a table and counting the shoe down from afar (also known as "backcounting"), and sitting down to play (wonging in) only when the TC goes sufficiently positive (+1 or +2, for instance). Then, when the TC falls below a certain number (like −2 or −3), you get up (wong out) in search of another positive count at a different table. This way, you only play games in which you have a positive expectation; eliminating playing through many negative counts makes you much more money in the long run. Plus, since you're only at the table during higher counts, you can launch out with a barrage of big bets, instead of varying your bet size and attracting unwanted attention.

There are a few things to take into consideration, however, in order to maximize your results. First, wonging works best in the larger casinos, where you have many more tables to choose from; that way, you don't have much down time when hopping from table to table. Plus, larger casinos give you protection; when you're constantly wonging in and out of games, you want to do so as anonymously as possible so as not to draw any undue attention towards yourself. Luckily, the average gambling masses are a superstitious bunch, so it is relatively easy to find a quick excuse to leave a table mid-game: a series of bad beats, for instance, or a fellow player who is playing his cards "wrong." You get the picture — any reason that will justify jumping out of a shitty game and into another high count at another table. Wonging works best when there are a lot of shoe games present, since shoes have the tendency to go positive or negative and then stay that way for longer periods of time (the running count may fluctuate wildly, but once the true count establishes itself as particularly positive or negative, it is much less likely to reverse itself quickly). Also, wonging is a great way to diminish potential heat, because you will not be in any one place long enough to make much of an impression on the pit critters or the surveillance staff.

## Wonging

The cool thing about wonging is that it allows you to act like you're playing on your very own blackjack team. One of the standard plays used by the big dogs of the famous MIT and Greek teams is called the "Big Player." It's done by using a player called a "spotter" who places nothing but minimum bets at a table until the count goes sky high, then surreptitiously signals in the "big player." It's that player who throws the monster bets onto the felt — and makes the real money for the team without drawing attention to anybody, since no one's employing wild bet spreads. Wonging accomplishes the same goal, as you act as both your own spotter and big player — calling yourself into the high counts, placing big bets to clean up, and wonging out when your advantage dries up.

Many casinos have adopted a "no mid-shoe entry" rule (as identified by table-top signs) to prevent this type of advantage play, which forces new players to wait until the next shuffle to start playing. Why the house doesn't just put up "No wonging" signs is beyond me, since the only players who are negatively affected by this rule are the ones who know what the term wonging means! Once you become even better at counting cards, you will be able to backcount two different tables at once, which gives you even more options as to what table to wong in on. At first it may be difficult to master the art of backcounting — especially counting down a table without looking like you are counting — but with practice, it will become second nature. Like riding a bike, it's something you never forget once you learn — and believe me, there are days when I wish I could turn off the switch that has me automatically counting down decks of cards when I am in or near a game. Now, if only I could remember where I put my car keys every night!

### Comp Hustling

You know you want it, you hustler you: free shit! Another way to gain an edge in casinos is by scamming your way into some nice comped suites, meals, and other goodies. This includes everything from free breakfast at the coffee shop to complimentary airfare and the famed RFB (room, food, and beverage) in which everything your heart desires is on the house. The secret to acquiring comps lies in simply understanding the formula casinos use in their calculations because, ultimately, all comps are just a percentage of the player's "theoretical loss" to the house — regardless of whether you actually win or lose.

What the casinos do is multiply your average bet by how long you play in order to estimate how much total action you're giving, then multiply that number by the house edge for the game you're playing to figure out your theoretical loss; finally, they'll comp you somewhere between 30–40% of this amount back in freebies (the specific amount varies by casino). Hence the comp room offers you receive in the mail and the free food and booze you get while actually on casino property. Got it? Theoretical loss (total action times house edge), multiplied by that particular casino's comp percentage (usually 30–40%) equals all the comp juice you can drink.

Here's an example:  Let's say you suddenly lose all sanity and play roulette like a champ for a couple of hours at $100 a spin.  If there are about 25 spins of the wheel per hour and you play for four hours, the total action you're giving the casino is $10,000 ($100 bucks a spin times 100 total spins in those four hours).  With a 5.26% house edge at roulette, your theoretical loss is $526, regardless of how much you actually win or lose while playing.  The casino will end up giving you somewhere between $160 and $210 in comps for your play that day at the roulette wheel, depending on the exact comp formula that particular casino uses.

Now you see how comp hustling enters the picture — apply the same formula to blackjack and suddenly you are getting "paid" comps for a non-existent theoretical loss. Since APs already know how to gain an edge at the game, any comps received are just gravy. I personally haven't paid for a room in Vegas for years because my comp power at many casinos in town is so high from all the time I've spent playing.  Comp hustling isn't relegated to just free rooms and show tickets, though.  It also includes using coupons that give you free bets, higher payouts on blackjacks, or giving you an ace as your first card.  The various types of comp hustling you can do are all discussed in detail in Max Rubin's book *Comp City.*  It's a valuable resource that every AP should study; until then, just be on the lookout for opportunities to hustle yourself some freebies — and don't be shy when asking for comps!

Usually, the casino marketing department will send you free room offers in the mail, but don't hesitate to call up and ask to be put up in a free suite.  If you are asked what "room offer" you have, you can feign ignorance and tell them you're not at home (aren't cell phones great?) and can't keep track of all the junk the casinos send you anyway.  While actually in the casinos, don't even *think* of paying for your own meals or amenities like spas or nightclubs — call a host and ask for a hook-up.  Emphasize what a good gambler you are, and how you just wanna have a good time, toss back some drinks, and hit the tables. You'll have your comp before the first drop of saliva can drool out of their mouths!

## The Great Player's Card Debate

Ah, to get a player's card or not, that is the question! Something to consider when hustling for comps, or just when playing with an advantage, is whether or not you want your play tracked by the casinos. On one hand, having a card opens the door to lots of comped rooms, food, and hookers — I mean, Booker's (a great bourbon that goes well in my favorite drink, the Manhattan). On the other hand, you have to give up all your personal information to get one, and will continually be harassed when buying in to tables without one: "Let me get you a player's card while you're playing, sir. It'll just take a few moments." If you do acquire one, you get tons of free shit, but the casino knows your real name and how to find you. If you don't, you generate all kinds of unnecessary heat every time you make up excuses as to why you don't want one ("I don't want to get stuck reporting this to the IRS, wink wink"), but you get to stay anonymous.

To be honest, there's no right or wrong answer here; it really depends on the stakes that you play and how much of a career you want to make out of advantage play. Total pros who are completely hidden in the AP underground would never play under their real name, but I usually do. I never went the route of fake IDs and the like, but have many friends who do. I wouldn't worry too much about it, unless you end up on a team or developing a series of other advantage plays (like hole carding, shuffle tracking, etc.). I haven't paid for a room in Las Vegas for years but, then again, if you end up playing with a multi-million dollar bankroll, you shouldn't really care about getting things comped anymore, right?

## Time for a Personal Story

Years after being barred from the Stardust, I still received tons of junk mail from the casino, including offers for free rooms and tournament invitational events. Before the Stardust was demolished, I received an invitation for their "Come on Back Tournament," a feeble attempt by the new owners to try to welcome back those who had been shunned over the years during the previous management's tenure (the Stardust always had a reputation for zero tolerance for APs). I decided to try it out, as I was already in town playing in a tournament over at the Hilton and wouldn't have to travel far if I was thrown out again. I intentionally waited to register in person until the day before the event, to provide the casino with as little chance as possible to put two and two together. I happen to be a holy terror on a tournament table, and wanted to slide into first place, collect my prize money, and get the hell out.

Well, it was not to be — as I handed over my registration postcard to the attendant at the sign-in desk, she immediately cross-checked my name against a magic list in her binder, frowned, and handed my postcard to a pit critter who was overseeing the action, pointing to the hidden list in front of her. He looked at me disapprovingly and pulled me aside, confidentially telling me that unfortunately I wouldn't be able to play in the tournament the next day and that he was "sorry" for any inconvenience. When I acted surprised and pressed him for a reason, all he could tell me was that there's a "short list" of names (read: long, long list of names) that would be unable to play, and that he didn't know the reason why.

I acted irate (hey, I really had nothing to lose, right?) and made it sound as if I had come to town just for the event. "I drove all the way from L.A. for this damn tournament, now I can't play, and you won't even tell me why? What kind of 'Come on Back' tourney is this?" I shouted, causing a scene, but of course he was just a tool of the system and could do nothing but stare blankly in my direction. Surprisingly enough, he hadn't thought to have security throw me out just yet, so I broke away from him to make the one advantage play still open to me before I escorted myself out: scarfing down a free lunch from the complimentary registration buffet. Prawns and champagne, yum!

### WHEN COUNTING GOES WRONG

Or, what to do when you get thrown out on your ass — and you *will* get thrown out on your ass! Hopefully not soon or often, but it is only a matter of time before you end up face to face with the business end of an underpaid pit boss's wrath. This is why it's so very important to train properly by using great discipline; the less you need to worry about the mechanics of keeping count, the more you can focus on the necessary evils of camouflage and your heat radar, giving you enough warning — and sense — to get the hell out before you are tossed out. Sure, you'll wear the first barring or two as a certain badge of honor — but after that, it's just no fun. To that end, here's the survival guide you'll need when they finally do come for you, when the hammer comes crashing down, when your check gets cashed, when your chips get colored up … and all that other metaphorical shit.

First, we need to differentiate between the various types of barrings you'll encounter on your journey. The mildest form of barring is called a "backoff" and is the nicest way to get fucked by the casinos; this is the equivalent of at least being cooked breakfast in the morning before being asked to leave. Backoffs are not actually out-and-out barrings, but rather when a pit boss or other casino suit "politely" tells you something along the lines of, "Your game is too strong for us. You are welcome to play any other game in the casino besides blackjack." What this really means is that they're pretty sure you're an asshole, but not so much so that your money's no good there anymore. They want you to know the gig is up, and if you're smart, you'll take off before things get any nastier.

This can be pretty intimidating at first, but quell your fear for a moment and realize that, by immediately leaving, you only confirm their suspicions about you. Make some protests, pretend to be flattered by their concern over you, act bewildered — then wander off to a craps table, a game they know can't be beaten. Moreover, if you really are an AP, they know you know it can't be beaten. So it goes a long way in your defense to spend a few carefree moments throwin' da bones before "getting bored" and finally wandering off; after all, although craps can't be beaten, it carries some of the best odds in the house, and the cover you gain by placing some small pass line bets (yes, "don't pass" bets carry slightly better odds, but you want to look like a gambler, not a pro) buys a hell of a lot more time with the surveillance team than the fraction of EV you lose by playing a negative-expectation game like craps. Just be sure you stay away from the cage on your way out, because, as I've told you, it's the best place for the casino to snap a nice, clear picture of you for their records — or worse, Griffin's.

I wish all barrings were as cozy as a simple backoff; unfortunately, things only get worse from here. The next level in the magical world of being shown the door occurs when you are unceremoniously "86ed." This is the kindest way of actually getting thrown out — Say goodnight, Gracie! — because it leaves open the possibility of your return. Sure, they'll harass and heckle you, rudely tell you to leave and never come back, and make you feel generally uncomfortable — but as long as you get out the door without having the Trespass Act read to you, the casino can take no legal action against you if and when you return.

Being 86ed (also a restaurant term employed when the kitchen is "out" of something — get it?) definitely sucks, but the third type of barring is one you really need to pay attention to: being "trespassed." This is when you are not only 86ed, but a casino representative officially recites the Trespass Act on your way out — it's kind of like the Miranda Act (you know, the whole "you have the right to remain silent" thing), but actually, it's legal mumbo jumbo for "Fuck off, don't come back, and if you do, we'll have your ass arrested." Fun stuff. This is the beauty of being an AP — we don't get arrested for card counting, we get arrested for trespassing.

Because casinos are considered private property, they have the right to decide who stays and who goes. Atlantic City is an exception, thanks to Kenny Uston's lawsuit back in the '80s. They can't throw a player out based on skilled play, though there are plenty of other ways to make an AP feel just as unwelcome. Regardless of whether your barring comes as a result of being 86ed or actually trespassed, you'll face the same type of hackneyed, tried-and-true militant ritual from the house, but being trespassed comes with the inherent risk of being tossed in jail if you return, rather than just tossed out.

As for what you'll actually go through when you're 86ed or trespassed, well, that's just no fun at all. Generally, it's a very organized event — think of it as a big send-off party all done in your honor — where a very firm, no-nonsense pit boss appears (or, if you're lucky, you'll get the hallowed tap on the shoulder) and before you know it, you'll be in the presence of some very stern security personnel while the pit critter tells you in no uncertain terms that you are a complete knee-biting jerk for being intelligent enough to count cards, that your kind isn't welcome here, and blah, blah, blah. The casinos have given this particular "test" a million times and they're pretty good at it by now, so there are several Universal Barring Truths to keep in mind in order to pass your "exam" with flying colors!

First, stay cool. You heard me; right now, you're probably freaking out, and that's exactly what they want you to do. Just chill out, take a breath, and relax. Remember, you're not doing anything wrong — and, more importantly, you're supposedly not even counting cards in the first place, you're just out having a good time. Right? Right. So step one here is to proclaim your innocence; this can be a very gray area, as you don't want to seem too insistent or adamant, but rather protest just enough to register your opposition without appearing belligerent or uncooperative. Along the same lines, you don't want to make any sudden movements — keep your hands exposed in a non-threatening, neutral position where everybody can see them. Believe me, those security guards are just waiting to toss your ass in a sling and back each other up on self-defense raps; after all, casinos don't take too kindly to having their bottom line threatened. Think of this little encounter the same way you would when a cop pulls you over for speeding and asks for your license and registration from the glove compartment; it's just a routine stop, but it could turn ugly if you get stupid. Sometimes you get lucky and there are no security personnel present, but trust me when I say they're on the way!

Your goal at all times should be to make it out the front door alive, and to aid you in your endeavor, chew on these truisms: It's illegal for them to detain you, force you to hand over your identification, or block your exit in any way — provided you act in a peaceful, complacent manner. Sure, they may try to stop you from leaving or make you feel like you're in "trouble" for doing something wrong, but as long as you are only being thrown out for advantage play, they have no jurisdiction over you save for escorting you out. At this point you have already proclaimed your innocence and should be clearly telling them something along the lines of, "Fine, I don't want any problems, I'll leave right now." Collect your chips from the table — yes, they are yours to keep, since you have not committed any crime — and walk slowly, deliberately, and directly towards the nearest exit while announcing your intention to leave so that there's no miscommunication and you get the attention of witnesses passing by.

Then, walk calmly out the door and do not even think about stopping at the cage to cash in. Not only is it the best spot in the casino to snap a good picture of you, but it's the one place where demanding identification is acceptable. Do not make any sudden movements that could even remotely be misconstrued as threatening, do not pass go, do not collect $200, and do not pick up a copy of the casino home game. Game over, folks. Have a friend come back on another shift to cash out your chips, or if you have to do it yourself, wait a day or two and do so in small increments. Then go chuckle about it all with your friends over a drunken game of mini-golf a week later.

Of course, it's not always this easy. I saved the best for last. You ready? The scariest and most insidious type of barring, hands down, is when you are "backroomed." The very word conjures up images of angry Mafioso enforcers taking turns on your stomach with big, meaty knuckles while a wiry Don pulls a Louisville Slugger out of a specially made violin case. Fortunately, the mob no longer has the same presence it once did in the casino industry — but there are still plenty of "legal" ways for them to fuck you up, don't you worry.

## Backrooming FYI

I have AP friends who keep the Gaming Commission on speed dial for these types of occurrences — and have been in a position to need to make that call in a hurry! Despite the fact that agents of the Nevada Gaming Commission (just like the courts, the police, and the politicians in Nevada as well) are usually completely beholden to the interests of the casino empire — hey, where do you think they get jobs after their tenure is over? — it still creates an awful lot of messy red tape to clean up after. As the old Yiddish saying goes, "When you need the thief, you take him down from the gallows." The same is true of the GC.

There are times when, despite your best efforts to leave the premises peacefully, an arrogant pit critter will demand you accompany him to a back room, and the team of security guards surrounding you interprets any move towards the door as an act of non-compliance. Sometimes, no matter how much you know your rights, you will be physically unable to leave; all you can do in this situation is repeatedly tell the assembled staff that you are not going to any back room, that you want to leave, and that if they insist on violating your rights, then they must summon the police and the Gaming Commission before you will move. Make a scene. Make it clear that you know they have absolutely no right to backroom you. And say a little prayer that this thing doesn't get any uglier than it already is. If you are forced into a backroom, shut the hell up, demand a lawyer, the police, and the Gaming Commission. Believe me, despite how beholden the GC is to the casinos' interests, the last thing the house wants is an official record of what's going on here. The path of least resistance for them is to just throw you out and try to scare you a bit along the way for good measure. Keep your chin up and you'll get through this all okay!

Perhaps one of the most important casino backroomings that has occurred in recent history is the much-publicized legal battle surrounding James Grosjean (author of *Beyond Counting*) and fellow AP Michael Russo, who together have probably spent enough time in casino backrooms to write an entire book on the subject — while actually in the backrooms. Basically, the two of them were hole-carding at Caesars Palace one day (a legal advantage play discussed in Chapter 3) when they were busted and, instead of just being 86ed or trespassed, they found themselves dragged into some horrible backroom under suspicion of card bending.

Before it was all over, they had both been arrested as card cheats based on trumped-up information provided by the Griffin Agency and Caesars's own surveillance files, and spent a few days in jail before the whole thing was cleared up. Well, you can imagine the holy hell that followed, as they spent years pursuing every kind of legal angle available to them. Unlawful arrest and incarceration is a pretty serious offense, but unfortunately in Nevada the truth doesn't usually matter.

Eventually, they won their case and both Caesars and Griffin were ordered to pay Grosjean and Russo each $25,000, as well as punitive damages. Caesars eventually settled their punitive damages for an undisclosed amount, and Griffin is now currently restructuring itself through bankruptcy proceedings to avoid paying the damages. But the blow has been struck, the precedent set, and as APs we can all rest a little easier tonight knowing that somewhere out there, real justice has actually been done, and the casinos may actually think twice before illicitly backrooming one of us once again. Well, we can hope so, anyway!

The last piece of barring etiquette you need to know is when it's cool to return to casinos from which you've previously been barred. Depending on how severe their initial response was, you can gauge how long you'll need to stay away before considering a reunion tour. If you've only been backed off, then I'd say you can come back a month or two later, albeit on a different shift. In fact, stay away from playing on the shift you were actually barred on for at least six months; the key here is to remember what the principal pit critter from your backoff looks like, so that you can make sure to avoid him in the odd chance he switches shifts on the day of your triumphant return.

After I was barred from the Stardust, I waited an entire year before trying to play there again (although I always used to make it a point to stop in to their Paradise Café for a late-night prime rib). I dressed a little more conservatively than my normal rocker self, and tried to sneak into the 21 pit. Well, wouldn't you know it — before I could even take a seat, there he was: the jerk-off who tossed me out a full year earlier. Damn mafia-looking chump. We made eye contact, and a glimmer of recognition passed between us before I turned and let the banks of slot machines swallow me up on the way to the nearest exit. Hey, if I still know what he looks like a year later, there's no reason to think *he* won't recognize *me* as well!

If you *are* actually 86ed from a joint, stay away for at least six months, and come back only with extreme caution (and of course on a different shift), most likely wearing some form of disguise. Seriously, man — you were lucky enough to get out the last time without the Trespass Act being read, so don't screw around with this one. However, in the event you have been officially trespassed from a joint, the best policy is actually to just never come back. I know a lot of people who wait a year or more and then go back in heavy disguise or with false identification (something many advanced counters have plenty of, but a topic I won't get into here), but the reality is, no amount of money is ever really worth getting thrown in jail over. If you really feel like the table conditions at the casino in question are so insanely good that you simply must return, then it's at your own peril. I wouldn't mess with it, but then again, that's just me. Do as you will — it'll be our little secret!

## FINAL THOUGHTS

I realize that all I've done these past few chapters is exhort you to be terrified of the creeping horror of the casino death machine, and you probably all hate me right now for being such an ass about it. But I must tell you, from the depths of my heart: It's all about love! I just want you to have the complete picture. A solid outline. The whole enchilada, if you will. To prepare you as completely as possible for the real deal waiting out there. And ultimately, the final caveat I offer is this: Have fun! Yikes, where did that come from? But it's true; if you've truly absorbed all the lessons herein, I am confident that you are ready to begin the fascinating, age-old game of cat-and-mouse with the corporate casino empire.

You are a spy in the house of love, a rogue agent operating so deep undercover that only you and a few whispered allegiances in the dark know the true depths of your mission. Embrace your calling, and enjoy every damn minute of it. Laugh off the heat as you run from casino to casino, burning the tables night after night. After all, the best way not to draw attention to yourself is to fit in as completely as possible with the ploppies: lost sheep in a wilderness of their own making. We must be the wolves in sheep's clothing, and rise above the shackles of ignorance to claim the rewards that are rightfully ours.

I think you're about ready, then. The collected wisdom of all my years in the trenches, making it happen for myself as a starving actor turned blackjack pro, is here. Grinding out the rent, keeping the lights on, taking out the ladies, stashing away money for a rainy day. Time to train up, strap up, and head out for your nearest casino — assuming, of course, they have any playable blackjack games left there. A dark day has fallen over the game of 21, and it's going to get a lot worse before things get any better. We can only persevere, and never stop enlightening everyone we meet to the dangers of casino marketing, 6:5 payout blackjack, and other gaming scams. Now that you've become a wicked sensei master of the art of card counting, I can only implore you to use your powers for Good rather than Evil. Because if I ever catch one of you fuckers lording your insidious card counting abilities over the heads of a band of starving Somalian refugee children — or being worshiped high atop a forgotten Greek isle as the dark god Standardus Deviationus, He Who Controls Variance — so help me, I will strip everything you have learned from your mind and banish you to an eternity of sub-optimal betting ramps in negative-expectation games. In fucking Antarctica.

But seriously, it starts now. You have officially been woken up from the long slumber of non-advantage play, and can never again return to that once blissful state of innocence. Gone are the days when the casinos played fair, the games could be beaten with "a little luck," and using your brain wasn't a crime (at least not in Nevada). Like that trippy surreal picture of Jesus we all used to look at in our misspent LSD-influenced youth (okay, well, that was my experience, anyway), once you see the blobs and colors suddenly snap together in the right focus and form the image of the Messiah, it can never be unseen. You are forever marked and changed. Go forth, multiply, and never gamble like an asshole again. You now have the key.

And — that's it. Put the book down and go make it happen. Seriously, dude, the rest of this book is pretty lame anyway. Just a bunch of fluff and filler my publisher forced me to write out of some hackneyed, antiquated "responsibility to my audience" or some other bullshit. I don't know what the hell he's talking about really. Besides, all I'm gonna do is harass, heckle, and swear at you fuckers some more. You might as well light the book on fire, return it, and try to get your money back. Claim irreparable harm or something. Talk about an advantage play! Fake a seizure while you're doing it, too — much more convincing that way. That's what I'd do.

Fine, don't listen to me.  Fuckers.

# The Bad Boy
# 7 of Blackjack
# Is Born

**Despite** countless trips to Sin City over the years, I had never really done the whole tourist thing — you know, seen some shows, checked out the fake volcanoes, etc. But that's exactly what I was doing one cold afternoon in December when I got *the* call: hanging out in the Bellagio conservatory with my best girl at my side and marveling at the large glass sculptures in the ceiling of the lobby. It's amazing how much money casinos will spend in an attempt to get the average patron to stop and spend all of his or her *own* money. Like we need to be tricked into spending it by the oh-so-confusing spectacle of sights and sounds. As much as I love the glittery gulch that is Las Vegas, the rank hypocrisy behind it all really makes me laugh. Imagine what Vegas would be if the casinos *really* had their way: New arrivals in town would be sent down a gaming-industry-regulated conveyor belt, injected with morphine and fitted with a feeding tube, only to be deposited roughly in front of a "Wheel of Fortune" slot machine in perfect *Matrix*-style, sci-fi precision.

But that's neither here nor there. The call I got was from Kimberly Holtzman, casting director for GSN (a hip, new incarnation of the old Game Show Network), and a terrific person who had cast me in a few game shows back in the day. A great way to make some quick cash as a starving actor in L.A. (aside from becoming a pro gambler, of course) is to land some spots on these lucrative blights of the television landscape! There's always room for another fun, energetic face on a game show, and the money you make on the back end is all gravy. My biggest win to date is $9,200 on a show called *Friend or Foe* that has a team of two players working toward a common bank, and then taking a shot at stealing it from one another at the end. Needless to say, I jacked my partner right in the mouth and stole the whole $9,200 from him. One day I'm sure I'll pay the karmic price for such rampant greed, but in the meantime — screw that guy.

Anyway, Kim remembered that I would list my occupation as "professional blackjack player" on the applications for these game shows, and as a result she and I had a few conversations about blackjack over the years. At that time, Game Show Network was in the process of changing its identity to "GSN, the Network for Games" and modifying its format to include more gambling and reality shows. One of its first original series was going to be the *World Series of Blackjack* and Kim was casting some of the world's biggest gambling authors to play alongside a few prolific upstarts, such as me, in the blackjack community. After a whirlwind series of meetings and interviews at GSN headquarters (which launched a great friendship with GSN Vice President of Programming Kevin Belinkoff, whose love for gambling in all its myriad forms is at least as sick as mine), I had been ordained as one of the 25 best blackjack players in the world and sent off to the Mohegan Sun casino to duke it out for ultimate bragging rights. I had arrived.

## Karma
In a curious twist of game show karmic fate, I used the free roundtrip airfare I had won on a previous GSN game show appearance to make the trip to the east coast and back for the filming of the first *WSOB*. Hey, what goes around comes around, right?

And where I had arrived was the middle of fucking nowhere. Due largely to the fact that Mohegan Sun is nowhere near civilization, I had flown into New York to have dinner with a friend (at an underground Manhattan sushi joint with great atmosphere but entirely overpriced spider rolls) before heading northward by rail. Grabbing my travel-worn luggage, I stumbled half-asleep to the exit and jumped out into the freezing Connecticut night. Snow swirled menacingly in the sky as it shot through quick bursts of nearby light. The cold bit into my hands as I shoved them deeper into my coat pockets. Gloves would be nice, but in the frenzy of last-minute packing back in sunny L.A., they had been, shall we say, neglected. Hair-styling products? Check. Punk rock outfits? Check. Tournament simulation notes? Check. Gloves? Shit. No gloves. Gloves are for people who live in places that get snow. And I am a goddamned Angeleno who will not be swayed by that bastard weakness of the flesh! Man, it sure was cold though. Mohegan Sun execs sure figured out the best way to trap patrons in the middle of nowhere with nothing to do but gamble their pensions away.

I finally settled into the warm and cozy leather backseat comforts of the waiting executive car and did my best impersonation of a guy who gets picked up by a manservant at a deserted Siberian outpost on a regular basis. And that was how I finally ended up at the door of the Mohegan Sun casino. It's a gorgeous, gorgeous building, both inside and out. Huge indoor waterfalls and gurgling streams wind around the interior of this spectacular feat of gaming architecture and ingenuity. Massive stone and glass "mountains" jut up uncompromisingly into the open chasm of space that fills this high-ceilinged gambling den. After I checked into my room, I went out to explore this lush paradise.

I wandered the casino floor, unable to play any of the games because GSN had warned all of the participants that Mohegan Sun reserved the right to disqualify us from the tournament if we played any live cash games while staying at the resort. There weren't any playable blackjack games available anyway — only monstrous eight-deck shoes with three decks cut off and unfavorable rules at which hoards of uneducated gamblers sat, vainly tossing their money away. "Where do these faces all come from?" I thought, thinking of Hunter S. Thompson's observation that these late-night patrons all looked like caricatures of used car salesmen from Dallas humping the American Dream, waiting for the image of the big winner to emerge from the pre-dawn staleness of a casino.

## F*&% Palace

Speaking of luxurious accommodations, I once played on a show called *Vegas Challenge* for the Travel Channel. It filmed at the Sahara hotel in Las Vegas, a relic of a place desperately trying to make a comeback. While I never could have predicted it, the ancient behemoth made an impression on me I'll never forget. Let's just say that the penthouse suite of the Sahara is everything you expect of a Vegas VIP suite, and more! Upon entering, you sink down into a plush living room complete with an entire wall made up of floor-to-ceiling windows and an array of lights hidden behind 1970s-style crystal beads. The master bedroom features the continuation of the aforementioned window-wall, but adds the classic presence of mirrors in the ceiling over the king-size bed. Aw yeah, baby! Finally, leaving nothing to the imagination, the connecting bathroom includes a stand-up shower stall large enough for 12 people and equipped with two shower heads on opposing sides and — of course — an entire glass wall that provides a sky-high, naked view of the Las Vegas Strip guaranteed to make even the most prolific practitioners of sexual perversity swoon.

The next morning, the contestants gathered for the first time as a group with various casino and television executives and production personnel to mark this momentous occasion in the history of blackjack by doing what all true and patriotic red-blooded Americans do to commemorate such a celebration of all that is good in the world of this, our shared sport: fill out lots and lots of legal paperwork! The cool thing about this otherwise anticlimactic activity was that GSN respected the fact that many of us used pseudonyms and wore disguises in public, and they went out of their way to protect our true identities. This was a major stipulation in the decision of many pros to attend the event, and even *with* this protection there were still many who shunned the limelight and turned down an offer to play, preferring true anonymity over a televised shot at $100,000.

I think most blackjack players will concede to the fact that the world's *true* blackjack champion is probably completely undercover and invisible to the rest of us. After all, the very nature of being a blackjack pro demands an absolutely clandestine sixth sense that prefers complete isolation over social camaraderie and professional association. Who needs to compare his gambling penis size when he's out making millions of dollars a year at some sucker backwater Malaysian dice bar playing a ludicrously profitable single-deck game? So forget all the Stanford Wongs, Anthony Curtises, MIT teams, and even mild-mannered (if there *is* such a thing) Hollywood Daves. The best blackjack player in the universe is undoubtedly a little Yemenite man named Solomon Q. Solomon, Esq.

GSN has always been a friend to the gamblers involved in its many casino-related shows; however, Mohegan Sun was anything *but* receptive to our being there. While their execs conceded to letting us wear our disguises and use our various pseudonyms on the show, we actually had all been pre-screened by the nefarious Griffin Agency so as to satisfy the casino that none of us were card cheats; apparently, the fact that we were all card counters meant that we were also in possession of questionable moral character. Although we were all cleared of any "wrongdoing," the negative stigma remained a constant throughout our stay there. Mohegan Sun was so nervous about having 25 "enemies of the state" in-house filming what was, essentially, a free, seven-week commercial for Mohegan Sun that security personnel followed us everywhere, so much so that we would often nod and say hello to our new "fans." GSN, of course, took many promotional photos of us for their own marketing, but we were all keenly aware that there were also more candid shots being taken of us by surveillance, always ready to believe that they could not turn their backs on us for a second for fear we would not be able to resist the temptation to slip some money onto the felt. I guess as a professional advantage player you eventually get used to being treated like a criminal for doing nothing more than using your brain to play casino games, but it certainly breeds a healthy amount of resentment.

GSN's hands were tied on certain issues, however — in order to allow the show to be filmed there, Mohegan Sun demanded certain concessions from the network. Chief among them being that no mention of card counting or other advantage plays was to make it through the editing process to air. Imagine that, a gathering of what the press release called "the world's 25 best blackjack players," and a complete gag order on any discussion of the skills that made us so knowledgeable! The next season of *World Series of Blackjack* was much more lenient, as GSN absolutely refused to allow the host casino to wield that type of creative control over the final product. As a result, many of us playing in the show's second season at the Golden Nugget in Las Vegas offered more than enough info on the subject of advantage play, and it made for better television. Also, to the Golden Nugget's credit, they realized the incredible marketing opportunity the series represented and likely gained much more revenue from the added exposure than they ever would have lost to a few advantage players trying their skills there.

## Damn Hypocrites

Embracing the true spirit of hypocrisy, the various casinos that have hosted the *World Series* events do not allow the participants to play blackjack on their property in their spare time. This restriction has a pretty curious effect, as after the tapings you can usually find a craps table overloaded with professional blackjack players, throwing dice and shouting like madmen! It's pretty funny to see a group of blackjack pros getting so excited over a game at which they know they'll lose in the long run. The sight of it would certainly confuse the living shit out of anyone from the Griffin Agency watching it go down. It also provides a great way for us to make fun of one another: One of the more well-known players in the blackjack community, known for writing computer training software, seemed to roll nothing but sevens and elevens on the comeout, throwing like eight or nine of them in a row. To this day, we still tease him by asking when his craps training program is coming out, since he's obviously cracked the secrets of the game!

No matter, though — in true renegade fashion, we struck a blow for advantage players everywhere during that long weekend of taping on the freezing plains of Connecticut. In what I can only describe as an egregious twist of fate, Mohegan Sun — the casino that had so reviled and feared us — decided in true bureaucratic fashion to give GSN a room in the executive office section of the resort for the express purpose of filming pre-game interviews with the contestants in a sound-controlled environment away from the presence of the annoying, incessant slot machines clamoring for attention. Wouldn't you know it, this space was conveniently located directly across the hall from the *Casino Director's* office! As you can imagine, those of us waiting in the hallway for our interview just couldn't believe how insane it was that some of the world's most notorious card counters were standing just a few feet from the nerve center of all that is holy in casino warfare. Lo and behold, at just that moment, an overworked network PA (that's "Production Assistant" for my non-industry-savvy readers; or, in layman's terms, "grunt," "lackey," "slave," or "bitch") decided to clear the hallway by turning that same Casino Director's office into a makeshift holding room! I mean, you couldn't have *scripted* it better!

We stood there in the office like kids in a candy store, imagining all the fun ways we no-good renegades could case the office for any and all information useful in our collective fight against the Evil Casino Empire. One of us could easily attack the computer, for instance, trying to find an open Griffin weblink or access to a password to aid in future scouting missions to that bastard site. The desk and bookcase could be cased for valuable bits of info, such as reports detailing the recent month's financial take from each of its table games, slot machines, and poker room. Perhaps papers titled "Suspected Counter Activity" with entries for the estimated amount of income lost to us bastard freethinkers would be found scattered haphazardly on the desk, undoubtedly as inaccurate as police reports that purport to list the "street value" of drugs seized in a big bust.

In any case, as we sat there with these visions dancing like sugarplums in our heads, a casino Suit walked by and casually glanced into the office as he went about on some errand. As soon as he passed, I snapped to the others and hissed "Hey! We've got heat!" At the same time, the Suit did a double-take and came back to the door — this time, pushing it fully open with the most curious expression on his face. Apparently, he didn't walk by fast enough, because a few paces past the office his brain had sluggishly registered an unthinkable "Alert! Intruder!" and he returned to confirm his worst fears. "What are you doing?" he stammered, incredulous at the scene before him. We fell in step quickly, striking confused images of mock repose. "Nothing. Some guy just told us to wait in here for our interview. Why?" I replied, challenging the Suit with our innocence. "You, uh, you guys can't be in here. I don't know who told you it was okay, but it's not," he finally proclaimed, ushering us back into the hallway. Just then, the PA who had originally given us this golden opportunity came out of the interview room across the hall. Salvation! He responded to the disapproving, unhappy look of the Suit by engaging him in conversation while the rest of us wasted little time disappearing around the corner.

## What the Hell?

At this point, you are either angrily gripping the book with white knuckles, yelling at me for not *actually* going through the desk, computer files, bookcase, etc. — or you are smirking somewhere on the inside, believing that everything I just suggested we *might* have done was *actually* done, and I just don't feel like going to jail today. So, how much of that little story was embellished? Edited to hell by my publisher against my will? Guess you'll just never know how much of a symbolic attack on the heart of darkness was done that day. ...

The rest of the taping went smoothly — except, in my not-so-humble opinion, for the eventual result! A *single card* separated me from being crowned the first World Blackjack Champion. Had the dealer busted her 15 on the final draw instead of pulling a 3 to beat my 17, it would have propelled me to the lead instead of leaving me in second place — but first-season winner MIT Mike was certainly a more than worthy Champ.

Let me say that, first and foremost, blackjack tournaments are a game of skill — with a helluva lotta luck thrown in to boot, I admit. And the first few *World Series* tourneys on GSN are true testaments to human ingenuity; while it is sometimes obvious that a certain percentage of participants are in over their heads, many of the players involved are really at the top of their field and true masters of the game. So good was that first season, in fact, that when I found out I'd be involved, I dedicated myself to re-learning every facet of the game before making my appearance at Mohegan Sun. I knew I was a worthy adversary and no stranger to blackjack tournaments (or cash games, for that matter), but these guys were the best of the best. The one thought that kept driving me through my studies was, "How am I going to get an edge over the very authors and pros that *taught* me how to have an edge in the first place? How does one go about gaining an advantage over other advantage players?"

## Study, Asshole

You don't get to be a rock star blackjack player without some effort behind the scenes — I spent an entire birthday once hiding in a hotel room studying tournament math and optimal progression ramps. My friends wanted to get me drunk for my birthday, but I was playing my second season *World Series* preliminary round the next morning and wanted to be at the top of my game. I even turned off my beloved cell phone to study in peace. I'll never forget the birthday cupcake — complete with lit candle — a fellow player sent up via room service just after midnight. No matter how much I wanted to go tear up the town, a blackjack player's work is never done. Study, study, study — there's always plenty of time to party *after* winning the green!

Mathematically, it just didn't make sense for me to go to Mohegan Sun and simply *hope* to outplay these legends of the game on their own turf while using their own rules and systems. It seemed obvious to me that, if I was gonna beat them, I was really gonna have to crunch every aspect of established tourney play I could and somehow, somewhere, find a way to innovate and improve upon what had come before. Develop a few secret weapons that no one had ever seen. After all, the one constant that *did* painstakingly emerge the more immersed I became in re-learning the collected wisdom of tourney lore, was that I now knew, without a doubt, *exactly* how my opponents would play. Which meant that the only variable remaining (and one would think this the most crucial point) is how *I* would play.

This realization led to the development of my own unique tournament strategy, which I began working on before the first season of *World Series of Blackjack* and have since refined, tested, analyzed, and perfected. The details of this labor of love, a more effective and responsive tournament strategy than has previously been available, would fill an entire other book, which I'm also considering having published. It is a much more technical book than the one you currently hold, and a must for serious tournament enthusiasts. Not only does it compile all of the strategies that went into my second-place finish at the first *World Series of Blackjack* (and many other notable wins since, such as the ones seen on *Ultimate Blackjack Tour),* months of improvements and refinements, and the collected wisdom of previously published books on the subject, it also includes a wealth of secret tips, tricks, and strategies employed for years now by the game's top pros that have never before been seen in print! And despite how much it sounds like I'm trying to whore myself (and my books) to you, I'm actually just trying to convey why I'm *not* going to go into further detail about all the strategy aspects of my play at the *World Series* here in this book. 'Cuz I could go on for 100 pages, and I have much more interesting things to tell you instead. Things like how Stanford Wong jinxed me.

That's right, the Godfather of Blackjack, author of all that is holy to advantage players, completely and totally jinxed me. I was so excited to meet him for the first time at Mohegan Sun, this man whose collected writings form the backbone of any good card counter's arsenal, that I went right up to him and thanked him for teaching me how to play blackjack. We chatted for a while and eventually I sheepishly asked him to autograph my worn-out copy of his book, *Casino Tournament Strategy*. When he asked me how I wanted it personalized, I told him the truth: to write, "Hollywood Dave — I taught you how to kick my ass — Stanford Wong." Well, he didn't appreciate the humor of that sentiment and instead wrote, "Dave — Good Luck and *I hope you come in second* (to me, of course) — SW." What a fucker. So you see, it's actually *his* fault that I didn't take the crown that year. A simple jinx like that, and BAM! Second place. But hey, I was serious when I asked him to write that I would kick his ass! I have many friends in the professional blackjack world, and even though there are several I absolutely dread playing against because I know what great players they are, whenever I *do* play them I am never shy about telling them how badly I am about to beat them!

## Causing Trouble

One of the cool things about these bigger tournaments is that they provide a great excuse for APs to get together and get into trouble. After a stressful day battling one another on the green tourney felts, it's truly wonderful to hit the town with some of the world's most notorious players! Once, a crew of hardcore shuffle trackers and I ended up at a blackjack table (in a casino that shall remain nameless), practically robbing the house blind. Now, while I understand the concept of shuffle tracking, I'm no good at it myself — but that didn't stop me from shoving out big bets whenever my compatriots signaled that the time was right!

After all, the first step in becoming the best tourney player you can be is doing whatever it takes to be better prepared than your opponents so that you have the best chance of winning, and combining *that* with the confidence of impending victory. Of course, it doesn't always work out that way, but if you don't believe in *yourself*, no one else ever will. Having confidence in your game both improves your chances of playing well and has the curious side effect of psyching out the competition. A large part of the edge I bring to the table with me during these larger tournaments and other televised games comes from having an attitude designed to give me a *psychological* edge over other players. It's one thing to have a great faculty for betting and playing strategy, but when playing with others who also exemplify this higher level of play, it is imperative to find any and all additional advantages you can, including giving your opponents the chance to screw up! In other competitive sports, psychology plays an important part of the game. Take a look at another popular card game, poker; dozens of books and hundreds of chapters within other books have been devoted to obtaining a psychological edge over your opponents at a poker table. Playing and betting your cards is one aspect of the game, but getting into your opponents' heads about how they bet and play *their* cards is quite another.

During the final table of the first season of *World Series of Blackjack,* for instance, I found myself sandwiched between MIT Mike — who had beaten me in round one, forcing me to win the wild card round in order to make the final table — and Kenneth Smith, one of the nicest, most humble, and mild-mannered people you've ever met. Ken's understanding of tournament mathematics is nothing short of terrifying. Although he and I had never met before, during the first few hands of the final match I casually leaned over to him and, after watching him surrender a hand (using the finger-slashing motion that also symbolizes "cutting your own throat"), I asked if he surrendered with the same hand that he masturbated with. Getting an incredulous look from him, I continued. "I write and surrender cards with my right hand," I said, "but I jerk off with my left." Finally (after I admittedly touched his knee inappropriately under the table a few times), the great Ken Smith busted out of the game! To be fair, I am sure my bizarre behavior alone was not the ultimate reason why he wasn't in contention come the final hand, but psychological warfare like this illuminates a much larger component of strategy than any mathematical analysis can shed light on. Plus, it's fun as hell!

That wasn't the only time I employed similar psych-out tactics during the *World Series of Blackjack,* though

I didn't always have to resort to such, shall we say, low
standards.  During the first season's wild card round, I
found myself in a tense last-hand battle with a player
known as Bobby J.  Everyone else had busted out, and only
one of us could advance to the final table.  I knew he was
a great blackjack player, if for no other reason than he
was part of the notorious Greek team, which has quite a
reputation for being one of the more elite and secretive
groups of advantage players making a killing extracting
profit from casinos.  However, blackjack tournaments use
a completely different set of betting and playing decisions
than do cash games — apples and oranges.  I knew he
would be vulnerable to cleverly disguised disinformation,
so I used a tactic with him that I have since refined and
discuss thoroughly in my tournament book.

# Blackjack Groupies

Blackjack 'groupies really *do* exist, my
friends. During the *WSOB*'s second season in Vegas,
a particularly "friendly" member of our studio
audience starting coming on to me during a break
in taping. Apparently, she really enjoyed watching
me play the previous round and made no secret of
her desire to get to know me on a more, shall we
say, *personal* level. Well, of course I was more than
happy to oblige my new fan (hey, what's a rock
star to do?!), but later was surprised to see her
putting the same strong moves on another member
of our blackjack cast! Before disappearing upstairs,
he pulled me aside and whispered, "Hey Dave, is
this girl a prostitute?" I could only smile and reply,
"Well, she didn't charge me!"

Part of my game is that I talk — *a lot* — during game
play, sometimes to distract other players who may only be
used to tournaments where talking is frowned upon, but in
many cases I am "talking out the math" of different decisions
— not only for myself, but for other players as well.  I'll
offer correct advice, sometimes to a fault, to opponents who
are considering their bet or play.  Often, they'll come up
with the same decision themselves, but occasionally they'll
think of something different and then have to compare

the two options. Whether or not they ultimately take my advice, I have already set myself up as a source of reliable information. In fact, many times I have given away *too* much knowledge by offering help when an opponent would have made a mistake. That's okay, though, because I am biding my time, waiting until the disinformation's really gonna count. Because I am reinforcing the *correct* decisions players make early on, I am able to psychologically do the same thing with *wrong* decisions, as well.

The trick to this kind of strategy is to *always* be thinking, quickly determining not only your own decisions but also the optimal (and, more importantly, sub-optimal) ones of your opponents as well. In the case of Bobby J, he came up with the correct bet to make on the final hand of our wild card round, and my own analysis of his bet gave him the reinforcement he was looking for. But come the second part of the hand, that of the playing decision, he was sitting on a total of 5, while I had a soft 20 and the dealer showed a very bustable 6. He had taken the low, betting small and forcing me to come over the top to win the game. Since the cards looked so favorable for me, he had no choice but to get more money on the felt by unconventionally doubling down on his 5. I knew this would not occur to him immediately, since in the cash games that are his forte it would practically be suicide. So as he sat and lamented his fate, I struck — reinforcing that yes, he had made the correct bet and how terrible it was now that he had to just hit his cards out to try and beat me. "If you double, I'll just double my own hand, so it really doesn't matter," I threw out, not relishing potentially having to ruin my great hand for something much worse if he did the right thing and doubled. Since his initial impulse was to agree with my advice, he hit instead of doubled, practically assuring me of the win I tasted just seconds later.

I have taken advantage of many other moments of disinformation during most of the big televised tournaments in which I've participated, but we gotta move on now, people. My ADD is acting up, and I feel like it's time for a topic change! Bottom line: Sometimes it pays to see things from everyone else's perspective and then give them back two-thirds of what they should already know. And, oh yeah, being part of the very first *World Series of Blackjack* totally kicked ass! I may be the same person I was before all the madness, but it certainly gave me the exposure I needed to launch so many other endeavors that are near and dear to my heart. Rock on!

# 8

## Celebrity Blackjack

**Well,** *someone* had to do it. If I didn't heckle Billy Baldwin on national television, I guarantee you somebody else would have — all in the name of good, clean American fun, of course. And nothing quite says "Americana" like that curious Zeitgeist of celebrity-themed gambling programming, GSN's *Celebrity Blackjack*. Although still a bedrock of such guilty pleasures as 1960s reruns of *The Newlywed Game* and *Match Game,* GSN decided to punk it out by adding blackjack and poker shows, billiards, even *Extreme Dodgeball*. And of course, the requisite celeb-riddled versions of each installment have become de rigueur. Enter Hollywood Dave.

After I turned in my second-place finish on GSN's 2004 *World Series of Blackjack,* the president of the network, Rich Cronin, congratulated all of the players for making the show a success. As I shook his hand after the final episode finished taping at 3 in the morning, I pulled him close and with my best actor-whore, guerrilla-networking chutzpah told him, "You know all of this was just one big audition to host one of your other shows, right?" Sure, I was happy as hell for the $30K cash prize and the recognition of my talents within the professional gambling community, but in my heart and soul I'm always an actor first and foremost. And damnit, I was ready for my close-up!

Well, not 90 days later I was back in GSN's Santa Monica offices thanks to Rich Cronin's decision that what their *Celebrity Blackjack* concept needed to separate it from the sea of other gambling shows on other networks was a smart-ass dealer and co-host. And, apparently, I was the smart-ass for the job! Combining the roles of zany host, expert commentator, and dealer all in one persona enabled the show to keep a fluid pace while still fulfilling the tenets of good casino TV structure. I was really excited by this pitch, because not only would I keep the cards in the air, answer questions, and dispense advice to the players, but I would have free rein to heckle, smack-talk, and joke around with the stars as well. I had done other gambling shows in the past, but nothing this fucking cool.

Here's a little-known secret, the unwritten first rule of celebrity gambling shows: *Celebs can't play*. Yup, you heard it here first, what you've long suspected but never had confirmed. It's true, no matter if it's poker, blackjack, or underwater knitting. I don't know about you, but when I watch most celebrity gambling shows, I just get pissed off — especially if I know something about the game. Which is why I thought *Celebrity Blackjack* was so much fun; no one acted as if these guys were *pros* — just that they love to play the game. Anyway, it's all for charity, which I think is an important distinction, since it frees up the players to crack on each other and just have fun instead of forcing the kind of manufactured, "in-depth" analysis you find on other gambling shows. Let's face it; people don't tune in to see Snoop Dogg play blackjack because they think he's such an amazing player. They tune in to hear him refer to his $17,000 bet as "one chip for each of the 17 true pimps out there watchin' right now." And I'm the first to agree that is *infinitely* more interesting to watch!

## It's a Tough Life!

In my opinion, the best parts of these shows were all the torrid onscreen love affairs between me and the many hotties I was forced to make out with. Hey, it's all in fun, right? I gotta say, the hottest kiss of all belongs to Shannon Elizabeth, who first came to attention for her role in *American Pie*, and whose duel with *The Practice*'s Camryn Manheim over who I thought had the softest lips (and tongue) left my head spinning.

To be fair, many of the celebrities on the show had a surprisingly good understanding of basic strategy, although the greater concepts of tournament strategy were often neglected. Then again, most blackjack pros have no clue how to play proper tournament strategy, either! A few players, such as second-season winner Jason Alexander, clearly had a stronger sense of tourney strategy than others, so he certainly deserved to win. At times, however, it was difficult for me to hold my tongue, such as when I was confronted with the simplest of playing errors. I can't tell you how many times I was asked whether someone should hit or stand on a 16, or the number of times people would forget to double down on their nines and tens.

Frequently, I *didn't* keep my mouth shut. After all, I had plenty of liberty to hurl fun expletives around and live up to my "bad boy of blackjack" reputation. I found that the longer we played, the more I would start correcting the guests whenever they made a crappy decision. While the importance of tourney play lies primarily in making the right *betting* decisions, I adopted a really bullheaded policy towards harassing the celebs into at least making the right *playing* decisions. I didn't want to present an irresponsible message to the home audience by not at least commenting when a bad play was made, so I had to make that compromise with myself at times. You can't just turn off good strategy because you're not actually playing the game, right?

All of the emphasis on keeping the game fun is what appealed to me the most. I think this original vision of the show is what makes *Celebrity Blackjack* stand out in a sea of gambling programming. What truly makes these episodes fun and worth watching are moments like Jason Alexander calling me an anti-Semite for beating the table with a badly timed blackjack, or rapper Coolio telling another guest — okay, it was me — that if I ever get a recording contract, he'll quit the business. Who really gives a shit that Lance Bass made a mathematically incorrect bet on the second-to-last hand? For that kind of analysis, there's *World Series of Blackjack*. *Celebrity Blackjack* is all about talking smack and taking names! And that includes keeping the language real and raw; many episodes were so laden with "bleeps" that for whole chunks of show, you couldn't hear what was being said due to all the swearing — like the time we started comparing the size of the guests' chip stacks to the size of their cocks. Before you knew it, everyone at the table was chiming in, making his own cock (and other assorted rooster) comments. GSN received plenty of complaints for what many audience members deemed racy or incendiary material (even though the show aired at 10 o'clock at night), but we were broadcasting from so very deep in cable, I don't think it mattered.

We got away with murder, as well as lines of dialogue that would never make the final cut on other networks or gambling shows. The overall attitude seemed to be a good-natured "Fuck 'em if they can't take a joke," and my role eventually developed into one of instigator. After a few minutes of my own crass heckling, the celebs would loosen up enough to pull out their own dirty wisecracks and take over. Caroline Rhea was absolutely brutal with the Baldwin brothers! Like the ringleader at a dysfunctional family circus, I would rile up the guests and then watch as the fireworks flew. And, oh yeah, maybe play a little blackjack along the way. Each show was its own party, and I had a blast at every one!

Despite such a permissive attitude towards the antics and views expressed on the episodes, certain bits were just too much, and inevitably fell prey to the editing process. Bad girl Shannen Doherty was fun and classy, against stereotype, but teen actress Bijou Phillips stormed off the set screaming obscenities when the producers asked her to take an exit a second time. Carrie Fisher was so far off her rocker that, at one point, she actually started crying and the show was paused for a moment while she regained composure. To be fair, she's a real sweetheart — but I don't think any of us knew if she was just *acting* messed up or if she was really that far gone. Adam Carolla went off on one of his trademark hilarious rants that unfortunately never made it past the censors. "I think it's great that you count cards, Dave," he told me, "but I do things a little different. I count 'tards. Because everyone else writes off the little retards out there in the world, and I really count on them. They make great license plate art and other valuable crafts, so I'm not gonna just cut them down and make fun of them like everyone else — I really count on those retards. So you keep counting cards, Dave, but I'm gonna count 'tards instead."

## The Tribe Has Spoken

Due to the magic of TV, we filmed two of *Survivor* host Jeff Probst's episodes back-to-back, and he ended up wearing the same shirt in both tapings. We had a blast teasing him on the second show, making fun of him for always wearing the same shirt when he plays blackjack. He eventually squashed it by coming up with some crazy *Survivor*-esque story about having washed his clothes in the bathroom sink.

One memorable episode involved comedian Richard Belzer, who participated in the first season. As is typical in the magical world of television, we were running late when the time came to tape his episode. Sometimes we would tape up to four different episodes a day and scheduling celebrities is a tenuous art at best. Usually, there were no major problems (unless you count Andy Dick getting trashed before his episode taped), but Belzer had a wedding to get to. It would've been disaster if he left in the middle of his episode or bailed out before the start of taping, because there really are no such things as "back-up" celebrities. After all, what celeb would wait around in a green room all day so he or she could gamble for charity, just to be sent home without playing?

To say we were as anxious to get the episode taped as Belzer was about wanting to leave was an understatement. Finally, in an attempt to at least make things look good, he started pushing max bet after max bet out on the felt so that he would bust out quickly. Well, instead of disappearing quietly into the night, he went on one the longest *winning* streaks I've ever seen! He won bet after bet, and when the betting limit was removed after the eleventh hand, he started pushing his entire stack of chips into the middle — and doubling up! By the last few hands of the game, Belzer had accumulated over *a half million dollars* in chips, and was a dominating force at the table! His next closest competitor had less than a quarter of the chips he did, and all Belzer had to do in order to win the match, and $10,000 for his favorite charity, was to sit back for six hands or so and bet the minimum, coasting into first place. But of course, you can guess what happened — after an incredible rollercoaster ride, he busted out two hands later thanks to a couple of bad $300,000 bets! With a flourish, Richard Belzer threw kisses to us all and vanished from the set.

Another personality who appeared on both the first and seconds seasons of the show was "Stuttering" John Melendez (of Howard Stern and Jay Leno fame), and we ended up really getting along with each other. One day, while trying to make a point about something, he illuminated one of the greatest fallacies of professional advantage play. The conversation concerned the correct way to play a certain hand, and I had a difference of opinion with someone else on set. John asked me if I had hit a million dollar score yet as a gambler, and when I told him I hadn't, he said that for as much as he trusted my training in blackjack, I must not be as good as I thought I was or I would've taken down a million dollar prize already. Believe me, that thought has constantly crept into the corners of my screwball brain since I started playing years ago. The truth is, it takes money to make money. Whereas I have lived comfortably for years, I make the same point to you that I did to him: Don't expect to turn a few grand into a million bucks overnight! It takes years of work and devotion, and since you profit only on a small percentage of your total investment, every dollar you spend out of your bankroll on other expenses takes away from the exponential gains you could have experienced. Set your own pace, be honest about your progress, and as long as you continue to profit on your journey, you are succeeding as an AP and can rest easy, million bucks or no.

Chynna Phillips stunned us all with her high-energy, come-from-behind victory in her first season appearance on the show. Actively channeling some form of ethereal spiritual aid, and admittedly without any kind of training whatsoever on how to beat blackjack, she used a bizarre strategy of nonsensical betting patterns and crazy antics to force the energy of the gambling gods to her side. She really embodied the true nature of hardcore casino gamblers, eschewing pure mathematical precision for some combination of voodoo, magic, and luck — and she won! So you see how little effect all the preparation, scientific study, and perfect play can ultimately have on the outcome of a game of blackjack. The truth is, *the majority of the game is completely out of our control.* There's no way to guarantee *anything* in the short run; all we can do is focus on long-term results. Over a day, a weekend, or single tournament, almost anything can happen — and usually does.

## Gamblin'

Daniel Baldwin is a raving madman, and God bless him for that. He and I ended up talking about sports betting, a kind of gambling that I've never really understood. He told me that he used to spend all his time in Vegas, and was a sports bettor for years. When I told him I never really understood how a pro could find enough of a reliable edge to make money in the long run, he broke down the formulas behind it all for me, using college football as an example. He was clearly very passionate about all of the minute details that go into sports betting, but it was all Greek to me and after a few moments, he lost me. "Wow, sounds really complicated; guess I'll stick to blackjack. You must have really cleaned up doing all that, huh?" I asked. "Oh, kid," he laughed, "I lost millions!"

Being an actor myself, it was truly an honor to work with so many incredible performers. If you would have told me when I graduated with my theater degree that I'd soon be on camera trading barbs with Jason Alexander, Kevin Nealon, Eric Roberts, Snoop Dogg, and the Baldwin brothers, I would have laughed out loud. For whatever reason, Hollywood has really embraced the gambling culture recently, so as a result of *Celebrity Blackjack* I've been welcomed with open arms into the entertainment industry. Not as the actor I came to L.A. to be, but as a pro gambler instead! It has certainly made my Hollywood path more interesting, to say the least. Rather than fighting the anonymity other actors rail against their first few years out here, I've been put on the inside track. Still, I must constantly remind everyone I meet that I'm "really" an actor. I've been classically trained in theater, have half of Shakespeare's canon memorized, and have performed in dozens of plays, commercials, independent films, and episodic television. Yet my greatest undertaking in Tinseltown to date has been waking up well on my way up the reality gambling show ladder. I've made some great friends, played in a lot of interesting home poker games, and ended up spending way more time than I should have at premieres, parties, and other wild Hollywood events. Funny how the world works sometimes, but ultimately we all play the cards we're dealt — and luckily for me, I'm loving every minute of it!

# Las Vegas Trip Report, circa 2001

**Early** in my blackjack career, I kept logs of my individual trips to the casinos, written out in a loose diary format called a "trip report." In the advantage player community, it is common for APs, fresh from a few days of play, to post a trip report of their experiences online so as to provide information and entertainment for other players. What follows is one of my earliest trip reports, dug from deep in the archives of my personal experience. My publishers have agreed to retain all of the original language, save for a few alterations made strictly for the sake of grammar and clarity.

I'm almost embarrassed to print it here, since you can very clearly see how much I had yet to learn about proper bankroll and betting requirements; in particular, notice how incredibly optimistic my RoR calculations are, as I write about playing $25 tables on a bankroll of just a few thousand dollars. It's a miracle I didn't go broke playing the way I did on this trip, but that's exactly why I wanted to include it here for you. It illustrates perfectly how someone, even after learning everything he needs to know about counting, heat, camouflage, and surviving in the casino environment, can still set himself up for failure by overbetting his bankroll. What's even more dangerous is that, since I was ultimately successful on this particular trip, it only gave me the confidence to *continue* overbetting my small bankroll until I eventually went broke a few trips later, and had to start all over again from scratch.

I encourage you to keep similar records of your first several trips as an official advantage player — if not in trip-report form, at least recall the basics of your session wins and losses and the corresponding table/heat conditions; in fact, many counters keep very detailed records of every session they've ever played. Not only does this provide a solid educational opportunity for you and other APs to compare notes, learn from one another's mistakes, and discover hidden profitable opportunities, but years later you'll have something to look back on of which you can be truly proud: a timeless account of the days in which you took your first few steps on the path to beating the casinos at their own game, and truly becoming a master at casino blackjack.

## TRIP REPORT

Well, my friends, another sojourn to the land of milk and honey! I was in the desert oasis of Las Vegas from September 29th through October 1st. I would've posted sooner but have been putting things in order back here in sunny Los Angeles for the past week. To business, then:

Arrived very late Saturday night, room comped at the Stardust and ready for some action. I brought about $1,100 with me and immediately went to work at the Stardust casino "warming up." My plan for the trip was to double or bust, playing only handheld games (using Hi-Lo for double-deck and Hi-Opt I for single-deck games), buying in for between $200–$400 a session (depending on the casino) and leaving when I had crapped out, won 50% of my buy-in, or played 75 minutes. My bet spread would be primarily $10–$40 (spreading to as much as two hands of $50 on monster high counts) and, being VERY youthful in appearance, my guise is that of the "happy-go-lucky, conversational, and friendly-yet-seemingly-naive college kid with big losses under his belt."

STARDUST: Down 300 bucks, losing my original buy-in after about 60 minutes of play. Sufficiently warmed up (and not feeling too bad over the loss; after all, I'm *staying* in this hotel, so why not make the house happy with some losses and make sure they keep the home-base comp RFB coming, right?), I headed downtown to the Horseshoe to start earning some real money. I usually have a comp

RFB waiting for me at the Horseshoe as well, but since I wasn't staying there this trip, I felt okay about taking their money.

HORSESHOE: Up $400 from a $300 buy-in after about 45 minutes; I was going to walk at $150 but the chips just kept rolling in. Some phenomenal splits and doubles on high counts paid off in textbook style. No real heat here, somewhat crowded, but I found a decent dealer who responded to my tokes with deeper pen. Gotta love Binion's!

CIRCUS CIRCUS: Coming back to the Stardust, I just had to stop at Circus Circus after reading about good double-deck rules variations, and rationalizing that this family hotel would be snoozing at 5 a.m. Well, I was right and pulled another $400 from a $400 buy-in. Again, in textbook style the chips just kept rolling in, although I had to use some more aggressive cover plays here as I wasn't able to entirely justify my otherwise typical counter profile by babbling excitable, naive statements about the action and my "dumb luck," because I was being watched from a distance. Again, I was outta there in 45 minutes.

STARDUST: Ah, home again to the Stardust. Bedtime called, but damn if I didn't sit down at my first green-chip table this trip for a quick nightcap. Now that my bankroll was above $1,600, I figured I could handle a more profitable $25–$100 spread. I swear, in 20 minutes I was up another $400 and left the table in glee, not wanting to push my luck any more. This time the pit bosses looked more concerned (I was sitting at one of their few "Stand on 17" tables and was spreading like I knew it; it was very late at this point and, while my count was still dead-on, my ability to cover competently was suffering. So I went to bed up $910 dollars, not bad for my first couple hours in town.

SILVERTON: Sunday was tournament day; the weekly 4 p.m. blackjack tourney down at the Silverton, that is. This was my first tourney and I was psyched. Even though I recently purchased Stanford Wong's *Casino Tournament Strategy* with the intent of sharpening up for some bigger games, I hadn't yet had time to do more than skim the material. Silverton has only a $20 fee, so I played the first 16 of 20 hands flat-betting the minimum bet, waiting for other players to crap out with aggressive play. Two players from each table advance to the quarter-finals and, unfortunately, I didn't make it. So I bought in for another qualifying round, and this time clinched the number one spot at my table. Because of my youthful appearance and erratic playing strategy, I often received well-intentioned, though unsolicited, advice on how to play "correctly" by the elders at the table. I usually love the attention because it fuels my naive cover as I eagerly accept advice and then continue to "get it wrong" much to my apparent chagrin. The Silverton was no exception; everyone there seemed to know one another and I was definitely the outsider. I qualified on this second round and progressed to the quarter-finals, then qualified there and went on to semi-finals. I would've made it all the way to the final table, but a simple math error on the 20th hand put me $20 shy of what I needed to land in second place. I kicked myself hard for that one, and overall it was a great experience, but after spending four hours there, I was more than ready to get back to the Strip!

BALLY'S DOUBLE DECK, green chip: Here's where my trip started to sour! About six weeks back, I caught some *major* heat at Caesars playing blackjack against a machine dealer, a pair of rooted critters, and some very unfriendly conversation. I escaped that session seconds from being barred. Well, then I went to Bally's — another Park Place (PPE) property — and handed over my player's card as I bought in for $500. I knew it was stupid to let them know who I was, but I had to know what level of threat PPE had placed me as in their system — I wanted to check their response. Well, I got it all right. Within minutes of the start of my play, I noticed a pair of critters eyeballing me while pretending to watch another table. The count went down and, since I was flat betting it out, I knew that I wasn't making any attention-getting plays. Imagine my surprise as a suit showed up and stationed himself directly at my table, staring me down. This guy was about 6' 2", as big as an ox, and didn't speak a word to anyone. Well, I played my session out and ended up losing the $500 buy-in — partly because the count never really showed promise, partly because I couldn't spread/play appropriately due to the heat. I should've walked earlier, but I wanted to fully gauge PPE's response. A lesson well paid for: PPE still didn't see my action as serious or high enough to bar me, but was definitely taking no chances. That's the last time I will use my PPE player's card; the flip side is, I know I have comp rooms waiting for me at the Flamingo, Paris, and Bally's due to my extensive play there in the past. [Note: PPE has since been bought out by Caesars, and most recently by Harrah's, one of the largest casino conglomerates in the world.]

Ah, CASINO ROYALE: This place was *packed* on a Sunday night and believe me, I stayed only long enough to use the 2:1 BJ payoff and the $10 match play coupons. Double deck with six other players is just no fun, and dumb luck was all I had going for me. I burned the match play coupon, unfortunately popping a blackjack with only $10 out. I saved the 2:1 coupon for another BJ when I had a higher bet out, but ended up leaving soon after without using it because I couldn't feel any sense of control or advantage over the playing conditions there.

Next stop, the HARD ROCK: God bless this hotel! Call it my demographic or whatever, but I just think that place is tits. I found a solid green-chip DD game with an amazing dealer who was giving me 70% pen after some decent toking. We struck up a lovely conversation, and when she went on break she went so far as to tell her equally hip break dealer to "treat me right." Well, the pen (and the tokes) continued. Only problem was, the counts were consistently low. I tried several bathroom trips, but could not get a solid advantage. Such a shame! The pit boss and I were fast becoming old friends as my buy-in slowly dwindled, which bought me some more cover and, of course, the pit boss loved me for it. The pen was 70% at its worst, occasionally rose higher, and I felt I could do no wrong. I anteed up another $500 buy-in, determined not to let my counter anonymity, low heat, and incredible penetration go to waste! Ah, stubbornness. $1,000 in the hole later, I finally called it quits, down $500 from my original $1,100 and now clearly with no business whatsoever at anything but a nickel table. Damn the devil Variance!

So, it was back to the HORSESHOE: Very, very late on a Sunday night and, like an old friend, Benny was there for me. I wonged like a madman; I table-hopped whenever there was more than one other player at my table; I played the part of a superstitious gambler to a "T" and YES, I had heat galore. At this point I couldn't afford debilitating cover plays or conservative betting strategies; I was on a mission to go to bed at least even with my original $1,100. And thank goodness, it all worked. But at what cost? My reputation has definitely been strained there, but at least I went to bed that night at peace with myself. Sometimes that means more than knowing the enemy thinks you're such a wonderful loser to have around. Too bad there's no way to mathematically factor in pride, huh?

As Hunter S. Thompson said, "There's a certain bent appeal in the notion of running a savage burn on one Las Vegas hotel, and then just wheeling across town and checking into another." [Note: As you can probably tell, this particular quote really stuck with me over the years!] Which is precisely what I did. Thanks to my incredible losses at the Hard Rock the night before, I now had a comp suite waiting for me. I'll say it again: God bless that casino! I just can't stay mad at them! So I checked out of the Stardust and wheeled back down to the Hard Rock before crashing for the night. No sense in passing up the larger room, and besides, the chicks poolside are much hotter there than at the geriatric Stardust.

TERRIBLE'S on Monday: A session at this place down the street from the Hard Rock ended up a farce. I had made a modest $60 on a $200 buy-in when a little old Asian woman in sweatpants decided to jump in on my game with her friend, both of them playing two hands. A decent heads-up game just splintered to five on one, so I took a walk. I started noticing prying eyes watching me as I sat on another table and continued to throw $10 bets around. Some additional joiners once again prompted me to leave, but this time there were two sets of eyes following me around. I dropped some dollars on roulette to cover myself, but sure enough, one eager boss decided to station himself right there at the wheel! There was no escaping the attention, but I was feeling particularly cocky at this point. After all, I wasn't really up that much and they were treating me as if I had some secret cheat on whether or not the roulette wheel was gonna pop up red or black! I see now that my mistake was buying in with $200 at this low-rent casino instead of the $20–$60 as is the norm.

I'd had enough of roulette and walked back to the first BJ table (now empty) and dropped my chips. The bosses followed me, and just as I was about to place a bet, out of NOWHERE the Asian lady and her friend bum-rushed the table, mumbling something about not wanting to play alone and immediately spread to two bets apiece before I could even play a single hand heads-up against the dealer. It was too comical; I yanked my chips off the table and, knowing that table hopping at this point would just land me 86ed for sure, hurriedly cashed out and left the casino before anyone had time to stop me. To top it all off, the apparently doped-up woman at the cashier's cage mistakenly counted my $25 stacks of nickels as $20s and almost short-changed me 50 bucks. I felt like I was in an old "Three Stooges" or "Laurel and Hardy" episode!

FOUR QUEENS: So, it was back downtown and this time, over to the Four Queens. The place was deserted, and I got some wonderful DD with phenomenal (80%) penetration. I bought in with $200 and made a quick $200, then left before they knew I was there. The boss had nothing else to do and had just started eyeballing my plays and bets when I decided to cash out. Interesting side-note: I took the side bet on very high counts a few times and won a little that way; I forget what they call the side bet there — "Lucky Ladies," I think — but it's the one where you get a 4:1 payout if your first two cards total 20. With a TC of +6 or more, you can pretty much bet on those faces coming — which is exactly what they did!

HORSESHOE: Instinct told me to stay away, but I just had to walk around the Horseshoe and see if I recognized anyone. Most of the personnel were different from last time (it was just before the 4 a.m. shift change), and so I hunkered down for a spell. But what happened next was not to be believed. The eye probably caught me, because moments after sitting down, an older break dealer I had not seen before, named Ed, came not just to relieve my dealer, but to actually "send her home early." No biggie, I thought, and anteed up. Suddenly, the pit boss started making comments to my dealer about not seeing him for a while and calling him "the Knife!" with glee. It was obvious that: 1) The pit boss had not ordered this break, and 2) Something unusual was going on.

Nevertheless, I played on and began to lose, often. It was crazy — this guy seemed to pull 20s and 21s like nobody's business, while I seemed to do nothing but bust consistently. At one point, I lost every single hand for three decks in a row! Thankfully, I was strictly flat betting $10. The insane thing was, no matter how low the count, the guy seemed to pull a never-ending string of face cards when he needed them, and I seemed to bust on every single 12 through 16 I held, no matter how low the count got. And then I heard it: the unmistakable sound of a second being dealt.

I immediately snapped to attention and watched from the corner of my eye as Ed sometimes (and usually) dealt/ hit by flipping the top card up and over, but SOMETIMES slid the card directly forward — accompanied by the scrape of two cards rubbing together against the dealt card. Well, I got the hell off of that table and planted myself at a roulette wheel with a direct sightline to Ed. And there it was: As he dealt to the remaining player at the table, I witnessed the BUBBLE PEEK and, inevitably, the seconds deal. I watched in shock as he cleaned out the remaining player, and then another player who sidled up. I was astounded; this was a first for me. Who knows if they've ever *really* been cheated, but here I was actually spotting and confirming it! Amazing. I got the hell out of there and will stay away for a long while.

[Note: The karmic justice here is that, a couple of years later, the Horseshoe was neutered by the gaming commission for an inadequate bankroll. It's true! In early 2004, the Horseshoe was forcibly closed by the state for several days after deputy U.S. marshals, IRS agents, and Metro police closed up the casino on a busy Friday night in order to seize nearly $1.9 million in cash from the tables and cashiers booths because of debts owed the pension and welfare funds of workers. This resulted in the Horseshoe's being left with less than the required level of cash available in the cage to legally stay open.]

HARD ROCK: I woke up the next morning and packed up, then went down to the casino to play my last game of blackjack for a few weeks ... and let me just tell you folks, once again: God bless this casino. In a little over an hour, I was literally SWIMMING in green and black chips. I had the same friendly pit boss keeping me company at an awesome green-chip DD game, along with one of the dealers who dealt the kick-ass pen from the other day. They could smell a "sucker" and genuinely liked my action, and as the count magically climbed higher and higher and my bets grew and spread to multiple hands, they cheered me on as the blacks started to fall in front of me. I managed to rat-hole away a few hundred bucks so as to not totally ruin a good thing, but not to worry. Whenever the occasional boss or shift supervisor stopped by to confer privately with the pit boss (apparently hearing from the eye that I was logging some substantial wins), he waved them off, letting them know that I was okay to play.

I finally colored up for a yellow ($1,000) chip and some change, and made my way to the cage. After my comp breakfast, I went back to the cage and cashed out the $400 I'd hidden in my pocket (just in case the supervisor called the cage earlier to verify that I had been paid only on the chips I left the table with). My total profit for the trip was a whopping $1,050 — give or take a few bucks — my target point. I made my way to the valet, grabbed my ride, and left.

# Intro to Tournaments

**Sorry** to disappoint you, but I'm not actually going to teach you a damn thing about how to win blackjack tournaments in this book. Yeah, you read that right: Suck on it, you bastards, but I'm not prepared to simply hand over that precious information just yet. I'm still using it in the casinos and on television, and you don't deserve the knowledge of my be-all, end-all advanced tournament strategy for demolishing every tourney in your sights. My publisher tried to get me to put in some sort of remedial tournament strategy chapter here, but I told him to go fuck himself. Why? Because there is no way I can summarize the incredibly complex series of decisions and considerations you have to make at every moment of a blackjack tourney in just a few pages, so I won't even try. After all, everything you've read here has been shot straight from the hip, without any sugar coating, so I'm not about to give you some watered-down crap and try to pass it off as real tourney strategy. I hope by now you realize there's no get-rich-quick scheme for the game of 21, so why should I start down the moral slippery slope into presenting some sort of "tournament primer" that attempts to give you a minimalist rule-of-thumb blueprint for conquering tourneys, like some other blackjack authors do?

So, why a tourney chapter here at all? To give you some sense of the incredible disparity that exists between playing tournaments over cash games. They're completely different animals, after all. In fact, the biggest mistake you can make is to assume, now that you've become a badass card counting AP, that you know something about tourney strategy. Trust me, you *don't*. I'll be honest: For as much as I know about making a living as an AP, there's nothing I do better than play tournaments — and it will most definitely take *twice* as much work to crack the code behind killer tourney skills as it did to cram true count conversions and the Illustrious 18 indices into your head. I don't want to let you loose on the tournament circuit unless you *really* know what you're getting yourselves into.

OK, fine — I'll admit I have selfish motives as well: The last thing I really want to do is teach anybody my secrets for destroying tournaments. Why? Simple. The main source of my current gambling income comes directly from various tournament spoils. Tourneys can be a very lucrative advantage play, and over the past several years, I've really cleaned up on the circuit. Many of you have probably seen some of my larger wins on different televised events. Due to the nature of these games — in which you battle other *players* rather than the *house* in order to win — the more educated the general public is, the more difficult my job. And therefore, the less money I make. And I'm not good at being broke.

As you can see, anything I teach you will only come back to bite me in the ass at some point down the road, since I'll inevitably be sitting across the table from you in some big million-dollar game and you'll use my advice to crack me. And then I'll be really pissed off and go on some long rant about how I never should have published my tournament strategy, how you owe me a cut of your prize money, and other ridiculously unflattering commentary. I hate to lose, so I'll probably kick over some chairs and threaten you with a calculator, just for good measure. And nobody wants to see that, right? Wrong; it actually makes for some pretty great television!

Lucky for you I love a challenge, so here's the compromise I'll make with you. I'll break down the history and major considerations of tournament play in this chapter, give you a full picture of what makes it such a unique discipline, and also why I love it as much as I do. As for the rest, well, let's just say I'll consider publishing it in the future. Until then, this is all you fuckers get. Deal with it.

## THE FIRST GREAT DAWN OF THE TOURNAMENT AGE

Ready for a quickie tournament history lesson? Good, I knew you would be. Believe it or not, tournaments are a relatively new phenomenon, first coming into prominence in the early 1980s. At the time, there was an incredible buzz in the blackjack world over this new trend; card counters and other advantage players came out in droves for what they perceived to be a casino free-for-all. They assumed they'd be able to crack the games without fear of getting kicked out, since in a tournament players are not trying to beat the house but rather, one another. Very quickly, savvy advantage players realized that card counting gave players little or no realistic edge over the game, and by the mid-'80s, a new breed of blackjack player emerged: the tournament pro. By discovering the hidden mathematical betting correlations and money management strategies that don't exist in standard cash games, these bands of early advantage tourney players were able to cut huge swaths of profit out of the new blackjack landscape, taking advantage of the general public's tournament ignorance, to clean up in event after event.

Eventually, these incidents would set the stage for what is now widely regarded as the first dawn of the tournament age: By late 1985, blackjack guru Stanford Wong organized and bankrolled a small crew of players (including Anthony Curtis and Blair Rodman) to mount an attack on the tourney circuit. Although certainly not the first such team of tournament pros, they easily became the most prolific. This was due, in part, to the fact that Wong used the group to actively test and hammer out the optimal betting and playing strategies he had developed with the aid of computer simulations and his own tourney calculations. This effectively created the entire early science of tournament strategy, spelled out for the first time in a mathematically sound language. Wong's seminal work, first published as *Tournament Blackjack* and now in print as part of *Casino Tournament Strategy,* is a necessary and indispensable text in the lexicon of anyone's tourney mastery.

Most notably, Wong pioneered an endgame strategy in *CTS* that incorporated some of the best hard-and-fast guidelines for betting and playing the all-important final hand of a tournament that would lead to the highest probability of winning. Two key concepts emerged here: first, that tournament strategy varies wildly from standard blackjack (basic strategy is secondary to the overriding betting concepts in play), and second, the awareness of the underlying correlative math governing not how often a player wins/loses/pushes against the *dealer,* but rather how often players win/lose/push against *other players* in contention. His work blew the door off the hinges of tournament strategy, for the first time publicly presenting the outline for success at the tourney tables.

True to form, Wong's crew and others who adopted similar strategies did major damage to the blackjack tournament world for several years, proving their mastery by exploiting all manner of tourney formats. For instance, Anthony Curtis won the World Matchplay Blackjack Championship, featuring a unique structure in which players shared the exact same cards every hand, the only difference being individual betting and playing decisions (two players would both be dealt an 11, for example, but one would be allowed to double down while another could simply hit instead) — a true testament to the mathematical skills of those who knew the most effective betting strategy to win the day! Eventually, like all good things, this first dawn of the tournament age faded, and with it the era of the first superstars of blackjack.

Unlike cash games, tournaments embrace a much more public aesthetic, so for the first time, those players who did well were openly recognized and rewarded for their efforts, rather than discriminated against and barred from play. However, with time, casinos got wise to the fact that the same key players were winning the majority of tournaments and — worried that their high-rollers would get frustrated by this tough competition and take their action elsewhere — started making it increasingly difficult for pros to find suitable games to play. Prize pools and equity (the ratio of prize money paid out to money taken in) went down dramatically; overlays (the money a casino adds on top of what participants have paid in entries) all but disappeared; and the total number of big-money tourneys available decreased significantly.

Perhaps the most notable evolution was that of the now commonplace "high roller" invitational, a sick brainchild offspring conceived by casino marketing departments in which a "free" tournament is thrown for the casino's richest blackjack players. After these high rollers bust out, they are then turned loose on the casino in the hope that they collectively lose back much more to the house than it paid out in prize winnings in the first place. The "purpose" of a blackjack tournament shifted from the pure game play aesthetics that had marked the games for so long to being solely a function of casino marketing departments' corporate greed. It is this bastardization of the tournament concept that marked the end of the first great tournament age and ushered in over ten years of true blackjack tournament hibernation.

One impressive development that *did* come about during this long period of hibernation, however, is the advent of a host of unique AP techniques used to extend one's longevity in the tournament world. Like cash game players employing camouflage skills to increase their time at the tables, tourney pros in the '90s had to find ways to get themselves invited to the lucrative free rolls while hiding their true identities as tournament experts, so as not to get blacklisted. Some pros adapted to this strange period in history very profitably, creating false identities for themselves and throwing around a lot of money on the blackjack tables until they found themselves regularly invited to these free events as big spenders, rather than advantage players buying in to a tournament. All change invites innovation and adaptation, and some players continued to make quite an impressive living during this hibernation period, despite the roadblocks created by an unforgiving gaming industry that is overly concerned with actively seeking out ways to limit the earning potential of those players who actually know how to consistently win.

## THE SECOND GREAT DAWN OF THE TOURNAMENT AGE

The present day, however, is fast becoming the second great coming of the tournament age. The night is always darkest just before the dawn, and it's no different in the tournament world. Despite how difficult it has been for many tourney pros to survive the past decade on tournament winnings alone, the pendulum is certainly swinging back in our favor due to help from a most unlikely source: television. The 21st century kicked off with a huge explosion in the popularity of televised gambling shows; you need look no further than the ridiculous saturation of poker into the collective social consciousness to see validation of this. And, after years of every imaginable variation on the poker format, the past few years have seen quite an impressive build in the presence of blackjack tournament action as well. GSN led the way with multiple seasons of *World Series of Blackjack* and *Celebrity Blackjack,* and many other networks followed up with their own tournament offerings as well. As I write this, CBS has picked up and is airing a minimum of two seasons of *Ultimate Blackjack Tour,* unprecedented network coverage in the world of blackjack.

The concept of gambling "celebrities" has become commonplace, and more information — and attention — is available on gambling and tournaments in general than ever before. As mainstream America continues to key in to this demand for more tournament television, casinos have no choice but to stand up and take notice. Like the incredible public outcry back in Thorp's day that made the entire gaming industry revert its blackjack rules back to a fair format, this modern-day explosion of gambling on television is creating an increase in blackjack tournaments with higher prize pools, as well as ones that are open not just to the general public, but to tourney pros as well. The road is slow, but the trend is definitely reversing itself.

What's also interesting are the many avenues that allow everyday players to qualify for competition on TV free rolls, with prize pools sometimes stretching into the millions of dollars. Players can now compete online for a chance to win a seat on the *Ultimate Blackjack Tour* on CBS, and casinos are following suit, hosting more tournaments to even more players than before, with better equity and overlays, in the same vein as the games of the 1980s. There's still so much ground to cover, but the future is once again bright for this sport. And as more of the old-school superstars of blackjack run into the New Guard gamblers (like my crew over at www.WestCoastGrinders.com), who have innovated the next generation of tournament strategy, it can only create more compelling television and, ultimately, the survival of the game, the theories behind it, and the continual growth of the strategies that keep things constantly fresh and exciting. Just like Wong's team twenty years ago, bands of new adherents can once again stay up late into the night, analyzing and dissecting optimal betting and playing decisions, formulating new thoughts and ideas for the future — now that there *is* a future. Needless to say, it's an incredible period of time to get into tourney play, and I for one have been fortunate enough to be at the right place and at the right time in history to catch an express ride to the top of this, the second great dawning of tournament glory!

## THE BASICS OF TOURNEY PLAY

First off, throw out your blind allegiance to basic strategy and the blackjack cash game strategy in general. I know, I know, you've spent months training, becoming a hardened machine capable of destroying the entire corporate casino empire in a single bound — pat yourself on the back and get over it; you aren't handed a card-counting medal when you show up in the afterlife. Besides, you're playing a *tournament* now, buddy. That means new math, new playing decisions, and a whole new approach to the game itself. As I've said, instead of playing the house, you're now playing against one another. Sure, the dealer may make a great hand and wipe out all of the bets on the table, but if you bet just $100 while your opponents all bet $500, that's the equivalent of your having just *won* 400 bucks.

Again, this is just an introduction and won't teach you what you ultimately need to know to make your mark in the tourney world, so please don't embarrass yourself by thinking for a second you can read the next couple of pages and then sit next to me at the final table of the *World Series of Blackjack* or some other major event and expect anything but obliteration. I'll smell your fear and inexperience from a mile away, which will only make me laugh and shake your hand for having gotten so far. For now, here are some key concepts of tournament strategy of which you need to be aware.

### Betting

Betting is what tournaments are all about. Make better bets than your opponents, and you will win more often than they do. Sure, luck plays an incredible role, but as I always say, "Fuck luck." It gets in the way of skill every time. Just like any other advantage play, results are best judged over time, as variance plays hell with any one single tournament in question. Some of the world's best tournament players go on cold streaks for dozens of games, only to experience several wins in a row. It's all about the long term, baby! There are many types of bets tourney pros use, all of which respect the mathematical odds of certain outcomes; the strategy for when and how to use them is the ultimate secret to mastering the game.

It's very important to remember that *at no time* should you ever place a random bet. There should *always* be a specific reason, a specific amount, and a specific correlation to other players' betting and playing decisions. Generally, when players are ahead, they try to "correlate" (match) their bets with what those behind are betting, in order to keep their lead. When behind, "contrarian" bets (betting big when others bet small, and vice versa) allow players to try to catch the swing they need to pull ahead. Other common bets such as "progressions" and "catch-up" bets work well to accumulate chips in a controlled manner, and "proportional" or "flat" bets involve simply betting the minimum, hoping others will lose more than you since, after all, the dealer beats players more often than not.

### Tourney Math

Remember the example I gave earlier when the dealer busts the table and everybody loses, but other players lose *more* than you do, so you actually win that hand because of the net gain in your total chip stack versus theirs? It illustrates why the whole concept of tourney math can be hard to grasp, because it is so fundamentally different from the regular casino version of 21. Who cares if the guy next to you goes broke or breaks the house in a cash game? All you care about in that situation is whether or not *you* beat the dealer. In fact, since you cannot get up and "cash out" the chips in front of you at any point during a tournament, they effectively cease to have a specific monetary value altogether and instead simply become the ammunition you must use to blast away at your opponents. Additionally, because the point of the game lies not in playing basic strategy, but rather in simply keeping a larger pile of chips than your opponents, tourney pros must regularly make the craziest plays in order to have the best shot of winning the game.

For instance, let's say it's the last hand of the tourney and you are heads up with one last competitor for first place; you are both tied and both betting $300. Now let's say the dealer gives you a 12, your opponent a 16, and turns up an 8 for herself; basic strategy says both players should hit their hands, right? Well, what happens when your opponent hits his 16, pulls a ten, and busts – what do you do with your 12 versus the dealer 8 *now?* Although BS would tell you to hit the hand, why risk busting yourself, and end up in another tie? Tourney math dictates that if you *surrender* your hand, you will lock up first place because by doing this there can be no possible result other than finishing with a $150 lead over the other player. Yup, do the math there — see it? You just don't screw with a guaranteed lock, baby!

Let's try another one on for size. You're down by $800, but the maximum bet allowed in the tournament is only $500. Again, you're in a heads-up situation, only this time you bet the full $500 and your opponent bets a paltry $100. And the same hands come out — your 12, the other player's 16, the dealer 8 — and once again, your opponent busts. *Now* what do you do with your 12 versus the dealer 8? Well, think about it — you're down by $700 (since your opponent with the $800 lead busted, losing $100) — which means that even if you somehow manage to win your $500 bet, you'll still lose the game by $200. So, once again, despite the correct BS play of hitting, the tourney math of the situation actually makes the only right play here doubling down. Sure, you've got to dodge the ten-value cards that would automatically bust you, as well as hope like hell the dealer either breaks or hits to a total you can beat, but *any other* decision you could make here results in a *guaranteed* loss. Only doubling offers at least a modest chance of success.

Figuring out the exact tourney math of each individual situation as it constantly changes with each hand can be an incredibly challenging, demanding, and creative skill. It's all part of the "fun" tourney pros get to have every game — forever evaluating the real-time, hard math odds of certain decisions granting marginally higher chances of success than others. Often, things aren't as cut and dried as these few examples illustrate, especially when you take into consideration multiple opponents, constantly varying chip stacks, and tournament structures. But, just as in cash games, at any given moment there's usually just one correct decision to make — and the strange and unique demands of tourney math governing these decisions fall out of the bounds of basic strategy much more often than not!

## Position

Just as in poker tournaments, the order in which you bet determines, in large measure, how effective your strategy will be. The later your position, the more mathematical information (i.e., other players' bets) you have access to, which allows you to tinker with your own bet amount and to take into consideration all manner of potential plays. However, being out of position and forced to bet earlier than your opponents can sometimes carry an edge as well, since you can size your bet in such a way as to force the more learned players (i.e., the Wong strategy players at the table, whose streamlined game play is often easier to predict) into making — or not making — certain bets in reaction to yours.

Position becomes most crucial on the last hand when, no matter what posturing has been made throughout the match, a single hand with a suddenly very finite, set number of mathematically possible outcomes emerges as the sole indicator of victory or failure. Having twice as many chips as your opponents is only as valuable as your position over them on the final hand; often, big chip leaders go down in flames simply because they cannot guard against shorter-stacked opponents who are able to make better bets and plays due simply to the value of later positioning.

## Chip Counts

What may seem like a forgone conclusion is often one of the most challenging aspects of tournament play. In a nutshell, to make the most of your strategy, you must take into consideration not just how other players are betting, but also how much in chips they have. While this may sound elementary, in the majority of tournaments, few — if any — allowances exist to access this information. While playing in a poker tourney, for instance, you can ask an opponent at any time how many chips he has left in front of him and get an accurate tally; not so with blackjack. Often, restrictive time limits (typically 30 seconds or less) exist to make a betting decision, and no help is given from players or the dealer when determining how many chips others have. Naturally, then, this creates the necessity for one of the most essential tournament skills of all: the ability to quickly and accurately count other players' chips by simply eyeballing their stacks, along with the mental acuity to retain this information as game play progresses, and adjust it as players win, lose, and push their hands. Sometimes keeping track of multiple players' fluctuating bankrolls can be quite daunting, but like everything in blackjack, this is a skill that can be mastered with plenty of training and discipline, and in time it becomes second nature.

Although I've personally sharpened my own chip counting skills well beyond the levels required for basic tournament play, I'm still a strong proponent of longer time limits and making chip counts more readily available to competing players. After all, it's one thing to have access to this information, and quite another to know what to *do* with it. I firmly believe that the loosening of these outdated, traditional devices can only create better competition. This can be seen in the myriad of TV gambling shows in which information on time limits and chip count are typically more generous and, as a result, the level of skill is truly allowed to shine. Like a great game of chess, I believe the focus of blackjack tournaments should be placed squarely on the player's ability to make the best betting and playing decisions based on the math of the situation, not the archaic data-gathering methods of yesteryear.

### Card Counting

Surprisingly, this skill is virtually useless in tournaments. The fact is, regardless of whether the count is highly positive or negative, all players at the table are playing with the same advantage or disadvantage with respect to the house, thereby leveling the playing field. There are much more important correlations that exist between betting decisions and the chip stacks of competitors, which far outweigh the benefits of card counting. For instance, if an opponent makes a move to catch up to you, your correct correlative bet would stand regardless of how high or low the actual count was at the moment. You wouldn't throw your lead away just because the count was low!

To be fair, legitimate arguments extolling the benefits of card counting do exist amongst the tourney pro community pointing to certain key times in a tournament where this skill can be useful. Some of these specific moments include when determining whether or not to take insurance or the best time to start a series of progression bets; however, the concept of variance is usually much more important than card counting in resolving these concerns. This means that, in a tournament situation, the decision to take insurance or make a larger progression bet is affected to a much greater degree by factors such as the relationship of your chip stack to other players' chip stacks, rather than the count.

In the same way that memorizing the Illustrious 18 indices alone does not give you 100% of the edge you could have by filling your head with hundreds of other index numbers, the ratio of actual advantage gained by counting versus time and energy spent applying that minor advantage is of very real consideration. There are many mitigating factors that determine how much variance you should be willing to accept at any given moment of a tournament, but suffice it to say that the count seldom has a strong enough relevance to make applying it worthwhile in the long run, especially since your time and energy should be focused much more profitably on other areas of the game instead.

## THE ROAD AHEAD

Historically, Wong's blackjack tournament strategies laid the groundwork for what many pros and most of the educated tourney-playing masses generally regard as the "right" way to play tournaments. Unfortunately, now that his ideas have been utilized by more adherents than ever, the math has finally started to work against itself. Although the heart of Wong's concepts will forever be universally applicable, the sad truth is that his theories were forged and solidified at a time when the general game-playing public was vastly ignorant of the betting concepts and strategy nuances that have since become much more common knowledge. Twenty years ago, using nothing more than Wong's strategies, a pro could take down just about any tournament in his path; this is no longer the case. Attend a modern big-dollar tourney and you will find the field littered with players whose general "Wong proficiency" and mastery of his *CTS* is at an all-time high. What this creates is an impossible paradox, and the question becomes simply: How does one *truly* get an edge over other players who share the *same* edge as you?

Gone are the days when one could steamroll over uneducated competitors with a mastery of betting correlations; sure, there are still plenty of cheap, local tournaments filled with tourney novices — but with prize pools that would hardly be worth a second glance. The *real* money games are now guarded by legions of the fiercest, mathematically Wong-savvy players that have ever existed. To gain an advantage over these pros, many necessary adaptations need to be forged in order to create an entirely new, hybrid, tournament strategy that is reflexive enough to react to the particular skill sets of those actually in moment-to-moment contention with you for the prize. What are you going to do when you sit down at a table full of *CTS* masters? The same thing as they do, essentially coin-flipping for first place? No thank you — I want an *edge*.

As of late, serious tournament pros have had to develop their own take on Wong's strategies in order to stay ahead of the game. I personally have developed what I believe to be the most comprehensive tourney strategy ever created, one that embraces all the math and foundations of what has come before, while providing a reflexive structure that adjusts in real-time to the unique present demands of modern tournaments as well as the higher skill level of modern-day competition. I am also considering publishing these strategies to share with the likes of you, even though you probably don't deserve such wisdom.

Unfortunately (for me, anyway), I'm sure that book would ultimately prove to be my undoing, as one day I'll undoubtedly have to face a table full of my readers who would proceed to make my life a living hell. Oh well, I'll cross that bridge when I come to it — and probably just force myself to come up with the *next* generation of tourney strategy as a result, and rewrite the books all over again.

I'll do it, too — don't tempt me, you bastards.  You'd think I'd have something better to do with my time, though!

Man, I really gotta get a life.

# KoV, UBT & the 11·
# Death of a Card Counter

**That's** right, you read the chapter title correctly ... it's done with. Over. Kaput. I've finally reached the apex of my career as a card counter, and the verdict is in: Playing advantage blackjack and copious amounts of television exposure do not mix. As this book goes to print, GSN is airing its fourth season of *World Series of Blackjack*, CBS is about to air the second season of *Ultimate Blackjack Tour*, and last year's *King of Vegas* still lives on in infamy. To say that this has increased my commercial visibility would be a serious understatement. You know it's time to hang it all up when you can't sit down at a blackjack table anymore without having a fellow player (or worse, pit boss) suddenly exclaim, "Hey, aren't you that blackjack dick from TV?"

## SPIKE TV BRINGS OUT MY INNER BAD BOY

The insane adrenaline ride that was Spike TV's first foray into casino programming, *King of Vegas* set out to crown not just the best poker or blackjack player, but the best overall gambler, period. To do this, executive producer and known sports bettor Wayne Allyn Root created a true gambling decathlon, wherein 12 participants had to prove their competitive mettle against one another through a myriad of casino games, including poker, blackjack, craps, roulette, pai gow, baccarat, and Caribbean stud. What made the show unique compared to similar projects I have worked on in the past (such as the Travel Channel's *Vegas Challenge)* was the added element of reality television. In this case, the producers were just as interested in exploiting the personality conflicts and character development between the competitors as they were in showing the nitty-gritty of split-second game play decisions. No other televised gambling show had ever followed this kind of formula; one minute the viewing audience was watching a tense final hand between players, and the next, cameras would follow a player offstage as he threw a tantrum over an unrelated incident.

While I felt right at home in this hybrid environment, many people were put off by this collision of concepts, wanting the show to be either 100% gambling or 100% reality TV, but not both. Despite the criticism from the professional gambling community, the show had quite a loyal following. The audience demographic contained fewer gambling purists, but attracted a more mainstream, entertainment-for-entertainment's-sake crowd. My bad boy persona really thrived in this curious mixture of genres, opening the floodgates to some of my more extreme TV moments and truly letting the other players have it — only when they deserved it, of course. Though I've never faced much resistance from the various networks I've worked with concerning the often coarse language and antics I've been known to employ, Spike TV (and, more specifically, the executive producer in charge of delivering the final product, Brian Gadinsky) made it very clear that I should feel as free as possible to explore whatever character dynamics I wanted during the taping of the series. A rubber stamp of approval from the man in charge to be as wild, crazy, and unpredictable as I desired? I felt like a kid in a candy store, all the while at the top of my game playing blackjack, poker, and other casino challenges in front of millions of viewers. Kindergarten was never this good!

So, in the pursuit of good, clean fun — and pushing the envelope as far as possible — I combined a razor focus at the tables with a penchant for obnoxious antics and lascivious table talk, using the different elements of the set as my own personal stage. At various times, I found myself climbing the steel girders that held up the lights (and falling off at one point!), jumping on top of the tables, going into the audience to sit (and flirt) with some of my fans, storming off the set in disgust after busting out of a round, and of course getting embroiled in some pretty dicey arguments with the other players. Steve "Chainsaw" Dempsey is a great guy and all-around gambling fanatic, but when the lights were on and the cameras began to roll, we had some of the most explosive confrontations ever seen on a casino show.

If one thing gets me going, it's when someone claims he doesn't need math, discipline, or training to become a gambling expert. At every turn, Chainsaw would mock my loyalty to the odds and percentages ruling every game, espousing instead a blind allegiance to unchecked aggression and dumb luck. For the longest time, our two diametrically opposed strategies held up neck and neck, and we would continually find ourselves advancing together to the next game, next round, and next episode. All the while, he'd be calling me a math moron while I'd be shouting about him being a brainless a-hole. A lot of people thought the constant fireworks between us would lead to blows on set, but it never went that far. Behind the scenes, we actually got along just fine — but knew that as soon as it was game time, all bets were off!

One of my favorite *King of Vegas* episodes came relatively early, as the Hollywood Dave/Chainsaw conflict really began to boil over, and the audience was just starting to love to hate me. I remember completely freaking out when a large population of the crowd starting cheering for him after he made some horrible play, got extremely lucky, won a ton of money, and then shoved it back in my face by saying something like, "Where's your fucking math now, Disco Dave?" Man, I literally saw red and started shouting to the audience that they needed to read, educate themselves, and learn how to stop dumping their paychecks to the house and finally start *breaking* the casinos like I do. I gave a whole impromptu gambling pep talk about how playing like a confident moron meant still playing with ignorance instead of knowledge, and I challenged every single one of them to step up, use their brains, and start taking it to the casinos. Luckily, this rabid speech made it through the editing process and was viewed by millions watching at home, which I considered a real victory in the fight against the casino empire. Knowledge is power, and if that rant got just *one more person* to open his eyes to the truth of advantage play, then all my bad manners are totally worth it at the end of the day.

Perhaps the coolest element of this series was the absolutely clandestine secrecy in which it was filmed. Not only were all 12 of us sworn to complete confidentiality about the project and its results, but we were also *sequestered* in our hotel during the two weeks of taping, much like members of a jury. This meant that we had very limited access to the outside world, and were not permitted to leave certain areas unescorted. At night we were confined to our rooms, and in the morning were required to sign affidavits acknowledging our adherence to these rules, with the threat of immediate disqualification hanging in the balance. As it turns out, losing a shot at a million bucks is a pretty good motivator! Additionally, we were not permitted to speak to one another outside of the taping studio — which made it a challenge to flirt with some of the hotties on the show. Nevertheless, I soldiered on, and what seemed very daunting at first actually became quite a badge of honor by show's end.

I made it through nine of the series's ten episodes, close enough to be able to really taste that money! And of course, beyond all the hype and spectacle, there was some serious gambling going on. To be honest, I had never even played some of the games featured on the show, like pai gow and baccarat. I have always steered clear of negative-expectation games such as those. So, like the true math nerd I am, I spent the days leading up to the taping devouring every piece of information I could find on each of the games. In many cases, this simply meant learning the optimal playing strategies for games I knew I would have no hope of winning in the long run; I could only expect to play better in the short term against my opponents, and combine that with superior overall tournament skill. Michael Shackleford's amazingly comprehensive gambling site, www.WizardofOdds.com, provided everything I needed to know in terms of the raw mathematical data behind the games I had to play, and from there I set about improvising my own unique strategies.

To do this, I fit the disparate risks inherent to each game into a standardized tournament mold; this meant finding the hidden correlations between the different games' bets and their mirror contrarian choices. For instance, I had the challenge of deciphering the optimal tournament play of the relatively mindless game Red Dog, in which players bet that the dealer will draw a card value that falls between their two dealt cards, receiving higher payouts for more difficult spreads. While figuring out the odds and payouts was easy, it was kind of difficult to determine exactly what betting ramps would best counteract the variables of other players' actions. To really bring my A-game, I wrote out pages of notes and charts for the *King of Vegas* games so that I would know the best way to optimally attack other players' bets and bankrolls at any given moment, including specifically how much risk I would need to embrace at any given moment. As tedious as that may sound, it's worth it when I can pull out some genuine creativity and get my hands dirty forming brand-new AP tools from the clay of the unprecedented demands of a whole new gaming environment.

## What Are the Odds?

When learning a new game, I've found that it's always much better to learn how to play it *right* rather than just simply how to play it. So, instead of learning all the possibilities available to me, I just want to know the odds behind each potential action, so that I can isolate my best bets, and know which I should hold in reserve for when I need a high-risk, big swing. To truly become a professional advantage player, one must visualize every game solely in terms of pure odds. At its core, any game of skill or chance is just made up of an escalating series of bets and payouts that are universally governed by mathematically-specific risks. So when you get right down to it, every casino game is essentially the same as every other game on the floor, each with its own unique set of odds. Some may be better or worse for the player, but ultimately, the math that binds them all together is exactly the same.

Ultimately, Spike TV spent more money promoting this show than anything they'd ever created in the past. Since I live right in the middle of Hollywood, it was pretty cool to see huge billboards for the series within a few blocks of my house. There's been an awful lot of talk about bringing the show back for a second season, but only time will tell. If it *does* return, look for the bad boy of blackjack to make a cameo — if only to harass a few of the new hopefuls along the way!

## UBT STAGES BLACKJACK COUP

Of all the blackjack productions I've been a part of over the years, I saved the biggest for last. CBS's *Ultimate Blackjack Tour* is the very first blackjack series on a major network, and is already a runaway hit. It's awesome to see blackjack finally grow up and join the ranks of the poker shows that have become such a prominent part of the television culture over the last few years. But what makes *UBT* so exciting is the particular kind of tournament being played, a brand-new, made-for-television format called Elimination Blackjack™. The brainchild of 1994 World Series of Poker champion Russ Hamilton, Elimination Blackjack takes the best elements of traditional tournament play and then tweaks it all out by adding secret bets and signature *forced* elimination hands, promoting a much more aggressive style of play. In traditional tournaments, the pros often sit around and wait until the last few hands to make key decisions, which makes for some unexciting TV. With this new format, however, the player with the lowest chip stack is eliminated from the game every eight hands or so, forcing the rest of the field to constantly get out there and jockey for position from the jump. A 30-hand tournament suddenly becomes an exercise in controlled surgical strikes, giving much more strategic importance to each and every hand, rather than just the endgame.

Most significant, however, was the field of players that made up the first season of the show. Currently, *UBT* is completely open to the public, but season one was a much more exclusive affair. Russ Hamilton gathered nearly 100 of the world's most notorious blackjack and poker players in a secluded location 20 miles off the Vegas Strip — at beautiful Lake Las Vegas — and held a week-long series of high-pressure Elimination Blackjack tourneys that would form the basis of the entire first season of the show. The majority of invited pros had collectively been banned from play at casinos worldwide, and together formed the single most impressive collection of blackjack players on the planet. It was truly an awesome — and humbling — experience to sit down at table after table of pro players, day in and day out, for a week straight. Never before had I been exposed to such an incredible level of competition for this long; GSN's *World Series* events had certainly prepared me, but this was most definitely the final exam.

## UBT Bling

In the world of poker, ultimate bragging rights are reserved for those who have won multiple World Series of Poker bracelets. Despite all of the other big-money international events out there, WSOP bracelets have taken a special place in the hearts of poker players everywhere. Currently, the three all-time bracelet leaders (Phil Hellmuth with eleven and Doyle Brunson and Johnny Chan with ten each) represent decades of achievement in the poker realm. And now the blackjack world finally has its own comparable system: *UBT* medallions! These gold and diamond necklace emblems are quickly becoming the standard for success in the tournament blackjack world. As this book goes to press, we just completed shooting the second season of *Ultimate Blackjack Tour*, where I won my second coveted *UBT* medallion — putting me in a four-way tie for first place in the race to own as many of these little suckers as possible! It's a long way to go to winning ten (or more!) of them, but I think I'm up for the challenge.

Once again, I found myself facing a very familiar, tough question: How do I get an edge over other top pro players? So it was back to the drawing board to search deep in my soul (and my math books) for the answers. I knew most of my competition would be at the peak of their game, but I felt reasonably sure that they would be at the peak of an entirely *different* game; that is, *non*-Elimination Blackjack tourneys. After all, this was practically the first time any of us had experienced this style of play, and by all accounts it demanded an entirely new way of looking at things.

So, just as I had done with many innovative events in the past, I spent weeks formulating a completely new way of looking at the game. I calculated different types of position-dependent aggression (the AgI, or Aggression Index), tinkered with varying bet ramps and their respective optimal progression charts, and ran countless real-time and computer simulations testing each new hypothesis. Finally, I got together with a group of other, edgier, mostly younger, pros to act as a sounding board for one another's Elimination Blackjack theories. Calling ourselves the West Coast Grinders, we applied similar aesthetics to our tourney strategies, which by this point were radically different at many points than the "accepted" theories of the older pros in the blackjack community. I hoped it would all prove to be the next step in the evolution of tournament strategy, and the ultimate proving ground now lay before me. And so I headed into battle.

## Preparing for Battle

Once more unto the breach, dear friends, once more;
Or close the wall up with our English dead.
In peace there's nothing so becomes a man
As modest stillness and humility:
But when the blast of war blows in our ears,
Then imitate the action of the tiger;
Stiffen the sinews, summon up the blood,
Disguise fair nature with hard-favour'd rage.

William Shakespeare
*Henry V* 3.1

At the end of that week of play at Lake Las Vegas, when the smoke finally cleared, I had qualified for two of the final tables to be filmed for television later that month in Los Angeles. Those two victories put me in an elite group of a scant few players who had achieved double-trouble status; most had been eliminated outright, while several managed to secure one precious shot at the prize money totaling more than one million dollars. As for the West

Coast Grinders and our similar unorthodox strategies, as a group of six players we had an unprecedented *seven* final table appearances among us. Apparently, we were on to something, and I have continued to refine these strategies into the powerful, reflexive approach to tournament warfare that I so humbly discussed in the last chapter. As far as that Golgotha in Lake Las Vegas, none of us walked away with any money for our efforts that week; however, the lucky few of us who fought our way to the final tables in L.A. were all guaranteed winners. At this point, it was just a matter of how much.

Arriving in L.A., I felt as if I had home court advantage. Whereas most qualifying players flew in from remote locations, the CBS studio is only a few blocks from my house. As had happened many times before, I had the advantage of having spent so much more time in front of cameras and under the hot lights than my opponents. Time to crank up the bad boy attitude and raise the psychological stakes to the breaking point! And, after another colorful week filming all the final tables, I had more than made my mark: a second-place finish, followed closely by a first-place finish, which qualified me for the championship table and a chance to play against all the other *UBT* first-place winners. All in all, these three final tables netted me well over $100,000 in prize money in just a few short days of shooting; also, my appearance at three final tables was tied by only one other player, *UBT* first season Grand Champion, David Matthews.

A fearsome competitor, David is one of a new breed of players who recognized early on that the secret to success in Elimination Blackjack tournaments lies in a much more aggressive style than is seen in other formats. I knew, every time I sat down at a table with David, that if he managed to get his hands on some chips, he was likely to go on to win the whole damn tournament; unfortunately (for me, anyway) he did just that. My punk rock hat's off to him — he's a more than worthy champ! Until, of course, season two and the return of Hollywood Dave ... (insert evil laugh here).

## GAME OVER

Don't get me wrong, I love the unique opportunities that being in the gambling spotlight affords me. But for every

TV series you see me on, another chain of casinos closes its doors to my play forever. Whether in the States, or across the ocean, the more attention I create for myself as a result of television (and other media) exposure, the less frequently I can actually ply my trade as a professional blackjack player. The sick, reciprocal relationship between

# Karma's a Bitch

On my second *UBT* final table, I made a side bet early in the game with poker pro Freddy Deeb. This happened as a result of my attempt to goad fellow player Skip Samad — a complete luckbox jagoff who had been unsuccessfully trying to steal my "bad boy" moniker — into making a $100 "last longest" bet right there at the table, in front of the entire viewing audience watching at home. This meant that whoever outlasted the other would win $100 from the loser. Although Skip had position on me (sitting two seats to my left, giving him a slight advantage) and insisted that he would beat me, he refused to take the bet. Well, Freddy recognized Skip's positional edge and agreed to take the bet on Skip's behalf —— for $1,000. Convinced my superior tournament skill would more than make up for any positional disadvantage, I accepted the higher wager. As fate would have it, a few hands before the last elimination round my chips had been completely devastated, while Skip sat on a monster stack created by an unstoppable series of insane big bet hands that had improbably won. Calculating my true odds of outlasting Skip at now less than 20%, I asked Freddy to let me buy out of the bet for $700. He agreed, and I immediately paid him. In true classy fashion, he promptly tipped our hard-working dealer $200. Well, in a whirlwind of betting, I not only ended up edging out Skip over the next few hands, but watched him go down in flames as I went on to not only outlast him, but actually *win* the match! The $50,000 prize made me feel good, but knowing I flushed $700 down the toilet for no reason still sucks ass!

these two extremes is yet another testament to the shallow hypocrisy of the casino industry, where famous poker players are elevated for their achievements while known blackjack pros only become more notorious and undesirable. Still, no matter the ethical divide, the result is the same: Game over. Thanks for playing!

So why did I pursue this path, against all sense? Well, at the end of the day, I still consider myself an actor and artist first and foremost, before all the card counting and casino bullshit. I'm constantly auditioning and taking meetings in L.A. for different non-gambling projects, and have been consistently popping up in commercials, films, and television shows for years. Yup, it's true; despite everything I've learned and continue to accomplish in the gambling world, no matter how far I've delved into the inner AP sanctum, I've always kept my eye firmly focused on the big picture. Hollywood, baby! Hey, they don't call me "Hollywood Dave" for nothing, right?

Of course, that doesn't mean I'll ever leave gambling behind. It's a part of me now, and there's plenty of good I can do from the other side of the anonymous cloak that insulates most of the AP community. All of the blackjack media coverage lets me say what can't be spoken by my card-counting brethren, giving voice to those who cannot speak for fear of being outed to the casinos. I had to face a tough choice all those years ago when I came in second at the *World Series of Blackjack:* whether to return to the obliviousness of the hidden AP trenches, or use this new exposure to start a ball rolling towards my future in Hollywood. It's no secret which side I chose, and to this day I look upon each and every television gambling experience not just as a shot at making money or furthering my career as a professional gambler, but as yet another "audition" on the road to success as an actor. Of course, now it's much easier than it once was; soon enough I'll dump a million bucks or more of my own money into an independent film and just do it all myself. I've always said that if I can't get in the front door, I'll go through the back. And if I have to take over the entire gambling world just to blow this door a little farther open in Hollywood, then that's exactly what I'll do! Besides, it sure beats waiting tables, right?

And you know what? I really dig the AP transformation

I've undergone over the past few years into being a tournament specialist. For as much as I love grinding away in the trenches, exploiting sick high counts while dodging the glare of surveillance Gestapo, there's a certain pride I get flaunting my passion for blackjack out in the open. How strange to be able to so vocally proclaim my love for the game, yet find this strange little niche within it that actually rewards that kind of PDA — public display of affection. Plus, I've discovered something pretty cool while following this particular path: The best moments in blackjack are the ones in which the turn of a single card is literally worth hundreds of thousands of dollars. In tournaments and on TV, it happens all the time — and there's just nothing like it. Win or lose, it's an eerie feeling to realize that all of the choices you've made in life have led to this specific moment, where the turn of one final card means so much. And the better you get at this game — or, some would argue metaphorically, life itself — the more chances you'll get to put yourself in that position, the place where skill intersects luck and training, preparation and opportunity. Clean living, my brothers and sisters, nothing but clean living.

"My gambling career supports my acting habit." - Hollywood Dave

One last thing. You know I'm full of shit, right? Well, not about *everything* — just the part about me not playing blackjack in casinos anymore. After all you've read, do you *really* think I would publish this book and pass up a chance to spread lies and disinformation about myself? It's called camouflage!

***

Actually, I'm just kidding. My career as a card counter is over. Seriously. Can't even take a hit on a soft 17 anymore without alarm bells ringing and an army of goons coming to drag me off into the night. Horrible stuff, really.

***

Come on! You bought that? In that case, I've got a bridge in Las Vegas to sell you! You know, the city I visit every weekend and plunder for untold sums of cold, hard cash? It's all true! In fact, I'm sitting at a table right now while you read this, splitting tens with impunity and glad-handling the cocktail waitress!

***

Sorry, didn't mean to make that up. In all seriousness, it really, truly, and most sincerely *is* over for me as a card counter. Why, just last month I went to Australia and got backed off before I even played a single hand. Flew across the ocean, checked in to the casino, and didn't even make it out of the hotel lobby before getting the tap. No fooling! I tell ya, it's just not worth it for me to even try anymore. I give. Uncle!

***

(wink, wink)

# Final Thoughts

**That's** it — I'm done with you guys for now. Time to toast the end of this book with a raid on the nearest gambling hall, a crazy party or two with some good people (read: cute girls), and of course, plenty of sweet, sweet bourbon. Make mine a Manhattan please, barkeep — and put it on the *casino's* tab. It's been a blast, my friends, but I most definitely have *got* to get out of here; too much blackjack on the brain can be a bad thing. And in that vein, I offer up one final thought for you. Never, *ever* forget the most important lesson of all, no matter how much you learn about conquering the game of 21 and no matter how mathematically brilliant your skills become: The most valuable advantage play you will ever experience is *the positive EV of human interaction.*

I sincerely hope you use what you've read here to become a living nightmare to the gaming industry, a thorn in the paw of bastard casinos everywhere; but, at the end of the day, it's never about the math, the numbers, the money, or even the pride of a job well done. It's all about the company you keep, the friends and family who support and love you, and the relationships that warm your heart and keep you strong. The more successful you become on your journey as a professional gambler, the easier it can be to lose sight of these things; after years of raiding the house, it can be tempting to reduce all the aspects of your life into simple mathematical expressions of EV. Find a balance; there will always be another game, another casino, and another advantage play to make. Don't ever be afraid to skip a night cracking a particularly lucrative shoe game for an important dinner, event, or connection with those most important in your life. Cherish every encounter, every person, every bond and relationship more than the highest count in the most heat-free game you've ever played, and you will open yourself to experiencing true happiness — something you will never find at a blackjack table, no matter how exciting or profitable the session becomes. And *that,* you can take to the bank! Cheers, fuckers ... I'm out.

# Selected References

## Books

**Advantage Play for the Casino Executive** by Bill Zender. Understand advantage players from the casino's perspective.

**Basic Blackjack** by Stanford Wong. Contains detailed information on the effects of various casino rules and play options.

**Beat the Dealer: A Winning Strategy for the Game of Twenty-One** by Edward O Thorp. The book that started it all.

**Beyond Counting: Exploiting Casino Games from Blackjack to Video Poker** by James Grosjean. Creative exploration of non-counting advantage plays; hard to find, but a true classic.

**Blackbelt in Blackjack: Playing 21 as a Martial Art** by Arnold Snyder. Excellent presentation on the realities of learning to count cards; contains the Hi-Lo Lite system.

**Blackjack and the Law** by I. Nelson Rose and Robert A. Loeb. A collection of articles regarding the law as it pertains to playing blackjack.

**Blackjack Attack: Playing the Pros' Way, 3rd edition** by Don Schlesinger. A bona fide reference book with tons of useful information and charts for dedicated pros.

**Blackjack Blueprint: How to Play Like a Pro ... Part-Time** by Rick Blaine. Great tutorial on learning to count; detailed team-play techniques revealed.

**Blackjack for Blood** by Bryce Carlson. Teaches the Omega II counts; includes some great camouflage techniques.

**Blackjack Secrets** by Stanford Wong. Thoughtful book focused primarily on camouflage and cover plays.

**Blackjack Wisdom** by Arnold Snyder. A collection of entertaining and informative articles on blackjack.

***Bringing Down the House: The Inside Story of Six M.I.T. Students Who Took Vegas for Millions*** by Ben Mezrich. Dramatized account of the famous M.I.T blackjack team.

***Burning the Tables in Las Vegas: Keys to Success in Blackjack and in Life*** by Ian Andersen. Amazing analysis of how to think about camouflage and cover plays as a pro player.

***Card Counting for the Casino Executive*** by Bill Zender. Understand card counters from the casino's perspective.

***Casino Tournament Strategy*** by Stanford Wong. Classic text on tournament strategy for blackjack, craps, horses, keno, and baccarat.

***Comp City: A Guide to Free Casino Vacations*** by Max Rubin. The authority on how to squeeze every penny of freebies out of the casinos.

***Ken Uston on Blackjack*** by Ken Uston. Autobiographical account of a legendary player's battles with the casino empire.

***Million Dollar Blackjack*** by Ken Uston. Reveals some great plays, techniques, and stories from Uston's years as a team player.

***Play Blackjack Like the Pros*** by Kevin Blackwood. A thorough account of what it takes to become an advantage blackjack player.

***Professional Blackjack*** by Stanford Wong. Describes the Hi-Lo count; this book taught me how to play blackjack.

***The World's Greatest Blackjack Book*** by Lance Humble and Carl Cooper. Teaches the Hi-Opt I system, as well as other useful thoughts about the game of 21.

# Websites

**6to5blackjack.org** Just Say No!

**AdvantagePlayer.com** Online community of professional players and home of RGE Publishing.

**AllInMagazine.com** The coolest blackjack/poker magazine, featuring my column "Head Games with Hollywood Dave."

**Bet21.net** Play against me in online blackjack tournaments — if you dare!

**BJ21.com** Stanford Wong's online blackjack community.

**BlackjackTournaments.com** Ken Smith's blackjack tourney website.

**ClubUBT.com** Subscription-based site with big prizes and thousands of monthly poker and blackjack tournaments.

**HollywoodDave.com** My home online ... the bad boy of blackjack in cyberspace!

**LasVegasAdvisor.com** Online community, plus access to the best deals in Vegas.

**PlayUBT.com** The Ultimate Blackjack Tour online, with plenty of articles and interviews with yours truly.

**QFIT.com** Where to get Norm Wattenberger's indispensable training software.

**Trackjack.com** Up-to-date blackjack playing conditions on casinos worldwide.

**TwoPlusTwo.com** Online community for poker players; the best of its kind.

**VegasTripping.com** Anti-establishment Vegas site, the real deal; plus, a few articles from your favorite bad boy.

**WizardOfOdds.com** Incredible resource for the math and numbers behind any and every game.

**WestCoastGrinders.com** Home to young, edgy pro gamblers dedicated to playing with an edge while staying cool — in poker, blackjack, and beyond.

# Index

Russo, Michael 107–108

## S

## T

## U

## V

## W

## Don Schlesinger's
## Ultimate Blackjack Strategy Cards

These cards feature both an easy-to-use Basic Strategy and a cutting-edge Ultimate Strategy, and are suitable for casino play. Each 3.5" by 5" tri-fold card contains four charts of the most scientifically advanced blackjack strategies available to the traditional player. Powerful and easy to use, each chart maximizes your odds of winning at the tables or online. Included are detailed instructions explaining how to use each chart, which rules are better for the player, how the house edge affects your bankroll, and much more.

## Blackjack Attack: Playing the Pros' Way
*by Don Schlesinger*

This is the third and final edition of Don's classic tome, loaded with a stockpile of strategies, innovative analyses, and unique insights into the game. Updated from the hardcover with a brand-new Appendix D (featuring completely revised and expanded tables on effects of removal for playing and betting), *Blackjack Attack* answers virtually all of the thorny mathematical questions that have puzzled serious counters for years: optimal betting, camouflage, risk analysis, team play, systems comparison, and much more. This Ultimate edition contains new studies bound to intrigue even the most knowledgeable pro, including a complete re-examination of the late Peter Griffin's work on expected values, and the publication of the most accurate basic strategy charts ever devised.

For more information or to order,
visit GamblingCatalog.com
or call 877-798-7743 toll-free!